Nelson Mandela

Significant Figures in World History

Charles Darwin: A Reference Guide to His Life and Works,
by J. David Archibald, 2019.

Leonardo da Vinci: A Reference Guide to His Life and Works,
by Allison Lee Palmer, 2019.

Robert E. Lee: A Reference Guide to His Life and Works,
by James I. Robertson Jr., 2019.

John F. Kennedy: A Reference Guide to His Life and Works,
by Ian James Bickerton, 2019.

Florence Nightingale: A Reference Guide to Her Life and Works,
by Lynn McDonald, 2019.

Napoléon Bonaparte: A Reference Guide to His Life and Works,
by Joshua Meeks, 2019.

Nelson Mandela: A Reference Guide to His Life and Works,
by Aran S. MacKinnon, 2020.

Winston Churchill: A Reference Guide to His Life and Works,
by Christopher Catherwood, 2020.

Nelson Mandela

A Reference Guide to His Life and Works

Aran S. MacKinnon

ROWMAN & LITTLEFIELD
Lanham • Boulder • New York • London

Published by Rowman & Littlefield
An imprint of The Rowman & Littlefield Publishing Group, Inc.
4501 Forbes Boulevard, Suite 200, Lanham, Maryland 20706
www.rowman.com

6 Tinworth Street, London, SE11 5AL, United Kingdom

British Library Cataloguing in Publication Information Available

Library of Congress Cataloging-in-Publication Data

Names: MacKinnon, Aran S., author.
Title: Nelson Mandela : a reference guide to his life and works / Aran S. MacKinnon.
Description: Lanham : Rowman & Littlefield, [2020] | Series: Significant figures in world history | Includes bibliographical references and index. | Summary: "Nelson Mandela: A Reference Guide to His Life and Works covers his life and works. The extensive A to Z section includes over a hundred entries. The bibliography provides a comprehensive list of publications concerning his life and work."—Provided by publisher.
Identifiers: LCCN 2019056207 (print) | LCCN 2019056208 (ebook) | ISBN 9781538122815 (cloth) | ISBN 9781538122822 (epub)
Subjects: LCSH: Mandela, Nelson, 1918–2013—Encyclopedias.
Classification: LCC DT1974 .M23 2020 (print) | LCC DT1974 (ebook) | DDC 968.07/1092—dc23
LC record available at https://lccn.loc.gov/2019056207
LC ebook record available at https://lccn.loc.gov/2019056208

Contents

Preface

Over the course of his life, from his birth in 1918 until his death in 2013, Nelson Rolihlahla (which means "one who bends branches" or someone who disrupts) "Madiba" (his familial Thembu clan name) Mandela was many things to many people: son of a Thembu royal chief, student activist, boxer, lawyer, Christian, communist, African nationalist, traditionalist, husband three times over, father, terrorist, prisoner, human rights advocate, Nobel Prize winner, president, elder statesman, hero, and global icon. Through it all, he was also a man with human frailties and weaknesses like any other. His life and works reflect an important though troubled time in the history of South Africa in particular, and more generally, the history of the transition out of imperialism and colonial rule in Africa. Born into a context where ideas and practices associated with governance were imbued with racist and patriarchal hierarchies, Nelson Mandela rose up to help free a country from the tyranny of a white supremacist government to establish the foundations of a representative democracy and majority rule, and in so doing to help the world come to a better understanding of the need for self-determination and democratic values.

Nelson Mandela's life and work spanned a transformative period in South African and world history, and it ranged from the rural margins of the British Empire to the pinnacle of global leadership, and perhaps even beyond to iconic hero. It demonstrated a number of important historical lessons. First, his transition from a life embedded in the traditionalist ways of the Thembu people to that of a Western-educated, sophisticated urban politician follows many of the contours of processes of independence movements and decolonization. He not only imbibed the trappings of British colonial culture, he embraced its ambiguities and seized upon the dimensions that supported his agency and cause. Thus, Mandela took advantage of Christian mission education, British and Roman Dutch law, and European political ideals found in socialism and communism to empower himself and all Blacks to challenge the long-entrenched inequalities of the world order. Second, he showed that Western culture could be synthesized with African culture in a way that gave those marginalized by it greater agency, and that African cultures were therefore not static or ahistorical as many colonizers thought. His success also pointed to the importance of finding common ground among those who valued the equality and opportunity that could only be found in a nonracial society. Finally, the lessons of his strategy and tactics, which included primarily a political and diplomatic approach buttressed by the willingness to employ the armed struggle, challenged dominant views of him as a terrorist. His story will be forever important in creating a balanced view of history in which the oppressors no longer get to define the terms of a conflict.

What we learn from Nelson Mandela includes a number of significant dimensions of human history. First, we see how he valued and drew upon a diverse feature of global culture, his Thembu, Xhosa heritage. This informed not only his views on leadership but also his reverence for the history of African culture and its rejection of domination from outside, which informed African nationalism in South Africa and across the continent. We also learn about adaptability. His willingness to learn from and deploy lessons from a broad range of resources, such as Mohandas Gandhi's use of nonviolent passive mass resistance as well as the turn to training in sabotage and military tactics, show his remarkable and practical eclecticism. We also learn of the value of patience and tolerance for others through his long years in prison, and his willingness to forgive his oppressors in order to facilitate a peaceful transition to democracy. The nature of his personal sacrifices, and his willingness to place his role in politics and the struggle before family as well as himself, are also a part of his story. Finally, we learn about the qualities of statesmanship and leadership through his perseverance in the face of the many challenges that threatened to derail his efforts.

The focus of this volume and the alphabetical entries of people and places is their relationship to Nelson Mandela's life and times. For this reason, choices have been made to limit or exclude some areas that, while critical to South African history and politics, did not intersect quite so fully with Mandela as those listed. The volume therefore provides selected insights through a number of features. First, a map of South Africa and the region shows locations critical to his life experience. A chronology then provides a list of key dates and events over the course of his life. The broad contours of Mandela's life and how it related to important themes in history are then contextualized in the introduction. The bulk of the work is made up of alphabetical listings of important places, people, and events that constituted most of his personal and political life. In some cases, particularly with political developments or organizations such as for the African National Congress, the entries are more substantial than for individuals in order to provide more context for the events and activities that people were caught up in. The relations among these entries can be seen through the extensive cross-referencing of entries set in bold. The appendix provides excerpts from key speeches that Mandela

made and a document, the Freedom Charter, which illustrated the foundation of his political goals and philosophy. Finally, it includes an extensive bibliography containing a discussion about and listing of select works. These include sources that provide background and context to both the history surrounding Mandela's story and an understanding of the political perspectives that he drew upon in formulating his ideas. The bibliography also lists key works by and about Mandela in languages other than English to demonstrate the extent of the importance and popularity of his message. Among those included are translations into some of the indigenous languages of South Africa, including isiXhosa, Mandela's home language, and Afrikaans. An important part of the bibliography includes the works directly authored by Mandela, including his celebrated autobiography, *Long Walk to Freedom*. Finally, in keeping with the recent shift to digital information sources and the prolific expansion of the Internet, the bibliography includes a list of select, stable, and very useful websites.

As a historian of South Africa, I have been privileged to have learned many lessons from that country's past in the many years I lived and worked there, not least of which came from Nelson Mandela's life. I recall my first visit to the country in 1985 when widespread mass resistance had provoked P. W. Botha's government to declare a state of emergency. I could only ponder then, as I drove past Pollsmoor Prison in the Tokai suburbs of Cape Town where Mandela was imprisoned, what his future fate might be. Happily, I was able to witness the worldwide celebration of his release and the euphoria of the first democratic elections in 1994 that brought him to the presidency. I remain grateful to all South Africans for both their courage and hospitality. Recent trips to South Africa that have directly helped with this work would not have been possible without the support of dear friends, the Howie family, and the staff of various archives in South Africa including the University of the Western Cape Mayibuye Center and the Nelson Mandela Foundation. My thanks also to Dr. Eric Tenbus, Dean of the College of Arts and Sciences at Georgia

College for his support. I would also like to express my appreciation for the patience and support of the series editor, Jon Woronoff, and the commissioning editor at Rowman & Littlefield, April Snyder. Any errors or omissions, however, remain my responsibility. Finally, I would like to dedicate this work to Kieran and Elaine, my fellow travelers in love and life who have shared with me a deep appreciation of the beloved country.

Acronyms and Abbreviations

AAC — All Africa Convention
AAM — Anti-Apartheid Movement
ANC — African National Congress
ANCWL — African National Congress Women's League
ANCYL — African National Congress Youth League
COD — Congress of Democrats
CODESA — Convention for a Democratic South Africa
COSATU — Congress of South African Trade Unions
CPAS — Communist Party of South Africa
FRELIMO — *Frente de Libertação de Moçambique* (Mozambique Liberation Front)
GNU — Government of National Unity
ICU — Industrial and Commercial Workers' Union
IFP — Inkatha Freedom Party
MDM — Mass Democratic Movement
MK — Umkhonto We Sizwe (Spear of the Nation)

M-Plan — Mandela Plan
MUFC — Mandela United Football Club
NP — National Party
NRC — Natives Representative Council
PAC — Pan African Congress
RDP — Reconstruction and Development Program
SACP — South African Communist Party
SACPO — South African Coloured People's Organization
SACTU — South African Council of Trade Unions
SADF — South African Defense Force
SAIC — South African Indian Congress
SANNC — South African National Natives Congress
TAC — Treatment Action Campaign
TRC — Truth and Reconciliation Commission
UDF — United Democratic Front
UNISA — University of South Africa

Map

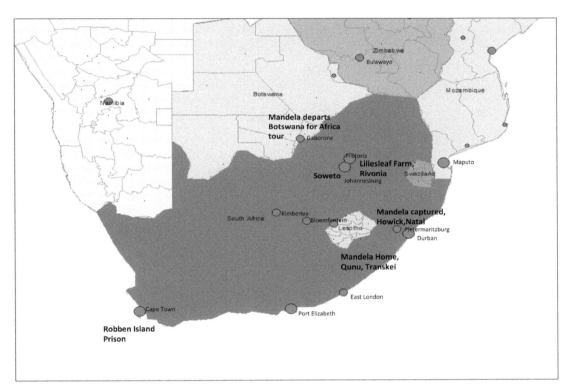

Mandela Map.

Genealogy

NELSON ROLIHLAHLA MANDELA (1918–2013)

Great Grandfather: King Vusani Ngubencuka of the Thembu (1790–1830)

Grandfather: Daligqili Mandela (na–1890); descended through the *Ixhiba* or "Left Hand" not entitled to inherit titles

Father: Nkosi (Chief) Mphakanyiswa Gadla Henry (1880–1930)

Mother: Nonqaphi Fanny Nosekeni (c. 1911–1968)

Marriages

1944: Married Evelyn Ntoko Mase (1922–2004). Divorced March 19, 1958.

1958: Married Nomzamo Winifred Zanyiwe Madikizela (1936–2018). Divorced March 19, 1996.

1998: Married Graça Machel (1945–).

Children

With Evelyn Mase

1. Madiba Thembekile Mandela (1945–1969)
2. Makaziwe Mandela (1948–1948, aged nine months)

3. Magkatho Lewanika Mandela (1950–2005, died from AIDS)
4. Pumla Makaziwe Mandela (1954–)

With Winnie Mandela

5. Zenani Dlamini (1959–)
6. Zindzi Mandela (1960–)

Grandchildren

1. Ndileka Mandela (1965—F—Thembi)
2. Nandi Mandela (1968—F—Thembi)
3. Mandla Mandela (1974—M—Makgatho)
4. Tukwini Mandela (1974—F—Makaziwe)
5. Dumani Mandela (1976—M—Makaziwe)
6. Zaziwe Manaway (1977—F—Zenani)
7. Zamaswazi Dlamini (1979—F—Zenani)
8. Zinhle Dlamini (1980—M—Zenani)
9. Zoleka Mandela (1980—F—Zindzi)
10. Ndaba Mandela (1983—M—Makgatho)
11. Kweku Mandela (1985—M—Makaziwe)
12. Zondwa Mandela (1985—M—Zindzi)
13. Bambatha Mandela (1989—M—Zindzi)
14. Mbuso Mandela (1991—M—Makgatho)
15. Zozuko Dlamini (1992—M—Zenani)
16. Zwelabo Mandela (1992—M—Zindzi)
17. Andile Mandela (1993—M—Makgatho)

Chronology

NELSON ROLIHLAHLA MANDELA'S CHILDHOOD AND EDUCATION

1918   July 18: Rolihlahla (translates as "one who pulls the branch" and means a troublemaker or agitator) Mandela is born in Mvezo in the rural Transkei area of the Eastern Cape to Nonqaphi Nosekeni and Nkosi (chief) Mphakanyiswa Henry Gadla Mandela, principal counsellor to the Acting King of the Thembu people, Jongintaba Dalindyebo. His father, Henry, was removed by a British colonial magistrate from serving as an appointed chief for having challenged the magistrate over complaints about a land dispute that Henry had adjudicated.

1923   The South African National Native Congress is renamed the African National Congress (ANC).

1925   Mandela attends the Methodist missionary primary school near Qunu. He is baptized into the Methodist faith and his teacher, Ms. Mdingane, gives him the name Nelson.

1926   Mandela's father, Henry Gadla, is dismissed from his official position as chief and headman, and the family loses access to the wealth and prestige that accrued to the title. The family moves to Qunu to live with his mother's family.

1930   Mandela's father dies and Mandela is made a ward of Thembu Regent Jongintaba Dalindyebo. He goes to live in the Regents "Great Place" at Mqhekezweni and is educated in the principles and protocols of African leadership and governance.

1934   Mandela undertakes customary Xhosa male age-set initiation retreat and circumcision ceremony; attends Clarkebury Boarding Institute in Engcobo.

1937   Mandela attends Healdtown, the Wesleyan College at Fort Beaufort and is introduced to British Christian-style mission education.

1939–1940   Mandela begins studies at the University of Fort Hare and is later expelled without earning a degree for taking a principled stand in supporting a student protest over the quality of the food.

JOHANNESBURG

1941   Mandela absconds to Johannesburg to evade a marriage arranged by his guardian, Regent Dalindyebo. He and his friend, Dalindyebo's son Justice, find jobs in security at Crown Mines and Mandela meets Black real estate agent Walter Sisulu. Mandela joins the Donaldson Orlando Community Centre to further train in his favorite sport, boxing. Later in life, his son Thembekile regularly accompanies him to the center to watch his father train and spar. Mandela also takes advantage of various entertainments in the big city of Johannesburg, including attending the cinema where he watches American gangster films. He also joins the multicultural International Club where he can socialize with Whites and South Asians. By 1943, he is made secretary of the club. Mandela also begins socializing with Yusuf Dadoo and other prominent members of the South African Indian Congress (SAIC) at their homes and in rented apartments in the Johannesburg city center.

1942–1943 Mandela completes his BA degree through the University of South Africa (UNISA) and enrolls in the LLB program at the University of the Witwatersrand. Begins working as an articling legal clerk at the law firm of Witkin, Sidelsky & Eidelman in Johannesburg.

1943 Mandela begins attending ANC meetings. Begins working with Ahmed Kathrada and the Cachalias, members of the SAIC.

1944 Mandela cofounds the ANC Youth League (ANCYL) with Walter Sisulu and Oliver Tambo.

1944 Mandela marries Evelyn Ntoko Mase— they have four children: Thembekile (born 1945); Makaziwe (1947—who dies after nine months); Makgatho (1950); and Makaziwe (1954).

1948 Mandela is elected national secretary of the ANCYL. The all-White National Party (NP) is elected and introduces apartheid, a legal system of racial segregation.

1950 Mandela is elected president of the ANCYL. The government passes the Population Registration Act, authorizing classification of all South Africans by race, as well as the Group Areas Act, which establishes country-wide residential apartheid, and the state begins forced removals of Blacks from areas designated as "Whites only."

1952 June 20: ANC launches defiance campaign. Mandela is elected as the president of the ANCYL and arrested and charged for violating the Suppression of Communism Act; is elected Transvaal ANC President; is convicted with J. S. Moroka, Walter Sisulu, and seventeen others under the Suppression of Communism Act. **July–September:** Mandela is elected first of ANC deputy presidents; opens South

Africa's first Black law firm to provide low-cost services to Blacks. He also begins studies toward a law degree at the University of the Witwatersrand in Johannesburg, but, owing to his involvement with politics and neglect of academic work, he did not complete it. **December 18:** Mandela is sentenced to nine months' imprisonment with hard labor, suspended for two years.

1955 June 26: The Freedom Charter is adopted at the Congress of the People at Kliptown, just outside of Johannesburg.

1956 Mandela is arrested and joins 155 other antiapartheid activists on trial for treason. The show-trial is a test of both opposition commitment in the face of serious government charges and of the state's resolve to defend apartheid. The trial gains international notoriety and spurs the foundation of the global antiapartheid movement, centered in London and the Netherlands. Although 120 of the accused are acquitted and released in the first months of the trial, Nelson Mandela and others are held over until finally released in 1961 on account of lack of proof that the ANC was a communist organization.

1958 Mandela and his first wife Evelyn Mase divorce after their estrangement, accusations that Nelson assaulted her, and after he had met Winnie Madikizela. Following the divorce, Mandela marries Winnie and they have two children, Zenani (born 1958) and Zindziswa (born 1960).

1959 Africanists who object to the ANC's growing cooperation with White and Indian people break away to form the Pan Africanist Congress (PAC).

POLITICS AND APARTHEID

1960 June 21: Police open fire on an unarmed crowd at a PAC demonstration against passed laws in Sharpeville, killing sixty-nine. The government declares a state of emergency and the ANC and PAC are banned. Chief Albert Luthuli and Nelson Mandela burn their government-issued passes in front of journalists. The ANC president Chief Albert Luthuli becomes the first African to win the Nobel peace prize. South Africa leaves the British Commonwealth. Leading supporters in the United Kingdom establish the Anti-Apartheid Movement (AAM) to place pressure on the South African government. Mandela is interviewed on television for the first time by British Independent Television News and the British government security intelligence services open a file on him.

LIFE UNDERGROUND

1960   July 2: Bram Fischer closes the case for the defense in the Treason Trial. In December, Mandela attends an underground meeting of the central committee of the South African Communist Party (SACP) national conference in Johannesburg. **December 16:** Zindziswa is born to Nelson and Winnie Madikizela-Mandela, the couple's second daughter.

1961   ANC launches armed struggle with Mandela and Joe Slovo of the South African Communist Party as cocommanders-in-chief of its military wing, Umkhonto we Sizwe (MK), or Spear of the Nation.

1962   February–August: Mandela embarks on his tour of Africa to establish diplomatic relations with African nations sympathetic to the ANC cause and to raise funds and for guerrilla training; he also attends meeting of the Pan-African Freedom Movement for East, Central, and Southern Africa (PAFMECSA) in Addis Ababa, Ethiopia. Leaving South Africa in secret via Botswana, on his way Mandela visits Tanganyika and meets with its president, Julius Nyerere. Arriving in Ethiopia, Mandela meets with Emperor Haile Selassie I, and gives his speech after Selassie's at the conference. After the symposium, he travels to Cairo, Egypt, admiring the political reforms of President Gamal Abdel Nasser, and then goes to Tunis, Tunisia, where President Habib Bourguiba gives him £5,000 for weaponry. He proceeds to Morocco, Mali, Guinea, Sierra Leone, Liberia, and Senegal, receiving funds

from Liberian President William Tubman and Guinean President Ahmed Sékou Touré. He leaves Africa for London, where he meets with Oliver Tambo and antiapartheid activists Mary Benson, reporters, and prominent politicians. Upon returning to Ethiopia, he begins a six-month course in guerrilla warfare, but completes only two months before being recalled to South Africa by the ANC's leadership. **August 5:** On his return to South Africa, Mandela is arrested at Howick in Kwa-Zulu Natal as he posed as a chauffeur for Cecil Williams, a White member of the Congress of Democrats. Mandela is sentenced to five years in prison for incitement and leaving the country without authorization. He restarts his studies toward a law degree at the University of London, but does not complete them there.

1963   July 11: Police raid the secret headquarters of MK at Liliesleaf Farm in Rivonia, north of Johannesburg and arrest the MK leadership. Mandela is serving his five-year term in jail for political agitation at the time, but is implicated by documents found at the farm in MK's Operation Mayibuye. He is charged with helping plan to violently overthrow the government and with planning sabotage.

PRISON

1964   January–June: MK leaders, including Mandela, are sentenced to life imprisonment at the Rivonia trial. Mandela makes his famous statement from the dock: "I have cherished the ideal of a democratic and free society in which all persons live together in harmony and with equal opportunities. It is an ideal which I hope to live for and to achieve. But if needs be, it is an ideal for which I am prepared to die." Mandela is transferred to Robben Island Prison where he will remain incarcerated until 1982; writes the manuscript for his autobiography *Long Walk to Freedom* (1994).

1966   September 6: Prime Minister Verwoerd is assassinated in parliament.

1976   June 16: In Soweto, state security forces suppress student protest movement against the required use of the Afrikaans language in Soweto.

1982 **April:** Mandela is transferred from Robben Island Prison to Pollsmoor Prison in Cape Town in part to facilitate the possibility of talks that could lead to negotiations, and in part to lessen his influence on a new generation of political prisoners on the island. **December:** The ANC escalates the armed struggle and begins a bombing of various government installations and offices, including magistrates' courts and a nuclear power plant.

1983 Oliver Tambo makes a radio address from the clandestine ANC station, Radio Freedom, calling on supporters to increase their efforts and to make the country ungovernable by the White minority NP government.

1985 **February:** In an effort to begin negotiations, State President P. W. Botha offers Mandela release from prison if he will publicly renounce violence and the armed struggle. Mandela, still unable to speak in public, responds through his daughter Zindzi, rejecting the offer and declaring only a free man can negotiate and questioning how he can accept while the ANC remains banned. **July:** Botha announces a state of emergency for twenty-six districts in the country.

1986 **March–June:** Botha lifts the state of emergency but reinstates it on June 11 as violence and protests in the townships intensifies, just prior to the anniversary of the Soweto uprising and extends it to cover the entire country. Over twenty thousand people are detained or jailed under the states of emergency. Mandela requests a meeting with Hendrik Kobie Coetsee, minister of justice, to discuss "talks about talks." Some ANC hardliners, on later learning of the meeting, object to what appeared to be unilateral decision to negotiate with the enemy without a party mandate and before the unbanning of the organization.

1988 **June–December:** International pop and rock stars, including Eric Clapton and Stevie Wonder, perform a benefit concert for the AAM at Wembley Stadium in London to celebrate Mandela's seventieth birthday. Later that year, suffering from tuberculosis, Mandela is transferred to Victor Verster Prison in Paarl.

1989 Mandela finally completes his LLB degree through the University of South Africa, over thirty years after he began it.

FREEDOM, NEGOTIATIONS, AND THE PRESIDENCY

1990 F. W. de Klerk lifts the ban on the ANC and Mandela is released from Victor Verster Prison on February 11, after twenty-seven years in prison. **April 16:** Mandela attends an international tribute to his freedom concert at Wembley Stadium, London. **May 10:** Mandela is involved in the negotiations leading to the Groote Schuur Minute, which laid out the agreement for the transition to democracy between the ANC and F. W. de Klerk's government. **June 1:** Mandela begins a six-week tour of Europe to present the ANC's plans for change. He then goes on a tour of Africa and gives a speech at the Organization of African Unity summit in Addis Ababa, Ethiopia.

1991 Widespread violence engulfs South Africa as a "third force" of vigilantes, supported by state security forces under F. W. de Klerk's NP government in transition, seek to destabilize the talks about a new government of national unity and a new constitution. Mangosuthu Buthelezi's Inkatha Freedom Party (IFP) supporters are discovered to be at the core of the perpetrators of violence. **July 28:** Mandela travels to Cuba to meet Fidel Castro and thank the Cuban people for their support of the ANC. **September 8:** Mandela gives a speech calling on all South Africans, ANC and IFP supporters, to "throw their weapons into the sea." He threatens to pull the ANC out of negotiations with the White government if the violence instigated by the "third force" does not stop. **September 22:** Mandela signs the National Peace Accord, which lays down the timetable for ending the violence. **December 5:** First meetings of the Convention for a Democratic South Africa (CODESA) are held.

1992 April 13: Mandela announces his divorce from wife Winnie Madikizela Mandela. The separation stemmed from her infidelity and criminal acts, which embarrassed Mandela and the ANC. **June 17:** IFP supporters attack ANC supporters at Boipatong, killing more than three hundred people. Mandela again threatens to halt negotiations unless the state-supported violence stops.

1993 Mandela and F. W. de Klerk, the last apartheid president, are jointly awarded the Nobel Peace Prize. **April:** Further violence erupts following the assassination of Chris Hani, leader of the SACP. **April 23:** Mandela visits the United States and urges Western nations to lift sanctions against South Africa in advance of all-democratic elections planned for the next year.

1994 March: An attempt to break away from South Africa is staged by African leaders and far-right White allies in the formed Homeland of Bophutatswana but it is put down easily by the South African Defense Force. **April 27:** ANC wins South Africa's first democratic elections, making Mandela the country's first Black president. **May 9:** Mandela assumes the office of the presidency and launches the Reconstruction and Development Plan (RDP) for the country.

1995 South Africa hosts with World Cup of Rugby tournament and Mandela presides over the opening game as a gesture of goodwill to Afrikaners, who were the major supporters of the sporting event. **April 10:** Mandela dismisses his former wife, Winnie Madikizela-Mandela, from her post as minister of arts and cultural affairs.

1998 July 18: Mandela marries his third wife Graca Simbine Machel, widow of Samora Machel, former president of Mozambique.

1999 Mandela steps down after one term as president. Thabo Mbeki beats out Cyril Ramaphosa, Mandela's choice to succeed him as the president of the ANC and heir apparent. The ANC wins a second democratic election with Thabo Mbeki as president.

2003 Mandela launches the Nelson Mandela Foundation, which focused on raising awareness of and combatting AIDS.

2004 June 1: Mandela retires from public life, leaving work as a mediator and counsel to the ANC.

2005 Mandela announces death from AIDS-related illness of his son Magkatho Lewanika Mandela.

2007 July 18: Mandela celebrates his eighty-ninth birthday and establishes the Elders group of former leading statesmen to assist in advice on mediations for world issues.

2008 April 30: The United States finally removes Mandela's name from its list of international terrorists.

2009 November 10: The United Nations announces the recognition of the date July 18 each year as Mandela Day.

2013 December 5: Nelson Mandela passes away.

Introduction

Nelson Rolihlahla Mandela was, for a time, more famous for what the world did not know about him than for what we now know of his complete life story. On August 5 of 1962, South African police, acting on a tip from the US Central Intelligence Agency, tracked down Mandela along a rural road near Howick, in the midlands of KwaZulu-Natal, some two hours' drive from the east coast port city of Durban. Mandela was accompanied by a White man, Cecil Williams. Williams, an ally in the liberation struggle for a democratic South Africa, was playing the role of a wealthy White being driven by his chauffer, Mandela in the guise of his apparently not-so-secret identity, David Motsamyi. The police, however, knew well by then who he was. Mandela was by that time seen as a notorious figure. He was known as the "Black Pimpernel" for his clandestine activities and, hitherto, his ability to elude the vast network of state security operatives that served the apartheid government of South Africa. He had also earned, in the eyes of most of White South Africans, the reputation as a radical communist agitator, and worse, in the eyes of the government, as a treasonous "terrorist" responsible for violent acts of sabotage. Following his arrest, Mandela made spirited, and now famous, presentations from the dock in two trials that set his fate. In the first, in October of 1962, Mandela appeared in what was a "traditional" Xhosa African kaross, a form of traditional dress representing his ethnic identity and ties to African nationalism. At his side, serving as his legal advisor (Mandela, a lawyer himself, served as

his own counsel, was Joe Slovo. Slovo was a member of the South African Communist Party (SACP), and so represented Mandela's alliances with a broader, nonracial opposition to apartheid. Mandela's intention was not to defend himself but rather to use the proceedings as an opportunity to press the case of the plight of all Blacks in South Africa who were suffering from the oppression and inhumanity of the apartheid system. The court sentenced him to five years in prison for agitating opposition to the state and for having traveled out of country—he had just returned from a clandestine mission across Africa to raise funds for his political party, the African National Congress (ANC), and to receive military training. While serving his sentence, Mandela was called back to court in 1963, this time to face far graver charges of planning the violent overthrow of the government and sabotage. Following his famous and impassioned "I am prepared to die" for the cause of freedom speech from the dock, he was sentenced to life in prison, though he managed to escape what many believed would be a death sentence. It was from that time, until February 11 of 1990, that Nelson Mandela dropped down the proverbial rabbit hole of the apartheid system and became at once persona non grata and an unseen icon of the struggle for political and human rights. Although for those twenty-seven years few even knew what he looked like, and his ideas were sequestered, he maintained all the passion and integrity of his commitment to his ideals. So, while his time in prison constituted a significant part of his life, he was able to contribute so much more before, during, and after that time than one would expect.

EARLY LIFE

Mandela's early life in the rural Transkei region of South Africa was shaped by the changing nature of African society in a colonial context. The demands of South Africa's unique industrializing political economy subordinated race and class to White domination, and from the 1880s, a pernicious migrant-labor system serving diamond and gold mining. These forces, driven by first Afrikaner and then British colonial settlers and South Africa's integration into the wider world of global capitalism, compelled Africans to engage with a new and rapidly changing set of circumstances in a decidedly unequal way. Nelson Mandela was born into a world where the dominant forces of White settler capitalism and industrial mining severely limited opportunities for Black people like him deemed to be worthy only of unskilled labor and service to Whites. Yet, despite these constraints, Mandela, and hundreds of thousands like him, found creative ways to challenge the system and fight for their rights. His father, Henry Mandela, for example, navigated the ambiguities that many African chiefs faced within the structures of colonial indirect rule. Employed as a subordinated, and some believed coopted, part of the colonial administration, "traditional" chiefs operated on a political tightrope, balancing the needs of their people against the demands of the White administration. In Henry's case, he ran afoul of a local White magistrate for trying to enforce Xhosa laws based on his sovereign autochthonous authority over a local land issue, and was dismissed as chief. So, Nelson was aware from an early age of the ways that the government could erode and corrupt African self-governance.

As he grew up in the Transkei, immersed in the customs and practices of his Thembu ethnic culture, Nelson came to appreciate many features of African life yet was open to new ideas and the wider world of the British empire. He learned to love and value the land that sustained the cattle he herded as a young boy. He revered the oral history of his people that highlighted heroic tales of past chiefs and kings and their valiant effort to stave off violent European conquest and he valued the transformative experience of becoming a "man" at the age of sixteen through Xhosa rites of passage and ritual circumcision. After his father passed away when Nelson was just nine years old, he went to live at the "Great Place" at Mqhekezweni, as a ward of the Thembu regent Chief Jongintaba Dalindyebo. It was there that he came to learn more about the history and qualities of African leadership that he claimed informed his later approach to politics.

Yet Nelson was not a person to cling to static traditionalism. His mother, Nosekeni Fanny Mandela, was Henry's fourth wife, but as with many African women living in traditional polygamous households, had come to embrace Christianity and the opportunities it afforded rural Africans for Western education and advancement. She was likely the key influence that allowed Nelson to take advantage of various Christian Mission schooling that would further empower him to navigate the complex world of urban life, work, and politics. His work at Clarkebury, a Methodist missionary secondary school in Transkei, from 1933 to 1935 and then at the well-reputed Healdtown Methodist College introduced him to formal education and also the customs and culture of the colonizing British. In his youth, he came to admire the impressive trappings of the leading imperial power, including a love for sports such as boxing and football (soccer), Western-style suits, and more importantly, the practices of debate and politics. With support from Chief Dalindyebo, a factor that most rural Africans could not count on, Mandela went on the prestigious University of Fort Hare where he studied anthropology, politics, and law. It was there that he also embarked on what would be his lifelong practice of challenging unfairness and the power behind it. At the end of 1939, Mandela was suspended from Fort Hare for his refusal to back down from his support of a student boycott of the food, which was perhaps more a matter of principle than substance. By that time, however, the burgeoning cities of

South Africa afforded young men more excitement and opportunity than the quiet rural villages of Mandela's youth.

JOHANNESBURG AND POLITICS

In 1941, Mandela and his close friend Justice Dalindyebo—his guardian's son—absconded from Chief Dalindyebo's home and authority. They fled from arranged marriages to find their fortune in Johannesburg, the largest city in the country and the center of both business and modern urban culture. The Johannesburg of the 1940s was a cosmopolitan paradox. It was home to countless exploited African migrant workers from across southern Africa who toiled in harsh conditions on the expansive gold mines, and also to the vibrant, American-influenced popular culture of African jazz and zoot-suited gangsters. It was a place of capricious racist laws that allowed police to harass Africans for just being there, but also offered countless "shebeens," informal bars, where Blacks could congregate and socialize. It was the heart of both White power over Blacks and the place where Black political activism could have a great effect. It was also the place where *Drum* magazine, and its White editor and later friend and biographer of Mandela's, Anthony Sampson, depicted the celebration of "modern" African culture in vibrant photo essays while most Africans were reduced to the most meagre of existences in wage labor, far from their rural homes and supports. It was, moreover, a place where courageous young Africans could sometimes win out against the odds and find opportunities to both advance within and yet challenge the system, as Mandela did. Mandela's arrival in Johannesburg, and the segregated African subcities of Alexandra and Soweto, in 1941, opened many new doors for the ambitious but principled aspiring attorney. As with many Africans who migrated to the cities, rural and kin connections sustained him, especially in the early days. A cousin introduced him to Walter Sisulu. Sisulu was an industrious real estate agent who built his business on helping newly arrived Africans find secure homes in segregated city. He also happened to be a member of the ANC, a leading Black political party with historic roots that was focused on combatting restrictive racist legislation and winning the vote for Africans. Sisulu helped Mandela escape the low-end job he had as a night watchman at Crown Mines for an opportunity to article with White lawyer Lazar Sidelsky's firm, and he introduced Mandela to the world of opposition politics. As he worked toward his law degree through the University of the Witwatersrand, which allowed Black students, Mandela also met and socialized with an array of leading "radical" political figures of the opposition. He met regularly at an apartment that hosted South African Indian Congress (SAIC) leaders such as Yusuf Dadoo and a young Ahmed Kathrada, and he went to parties where communists Joe Slovo and Ruth First befriended him. Through these connections, Mandela quickly learned about political parties and philosophies that not just opposed the racism and inequality of South African society but actually offered progressive alternatives. These included plans for practical mass protest action that harkened back to the work in South Africa of Mohandas Gandhi to organized socialist structures of party governance that could be applied to building a better government for all. Perhaps the greatest challenge facing him with such a dizzying array of possibilities was how to reconcile them with the core values, history, and cultural experiences of the majority African population. Despite his initial fears of White and Indian South African leadership eclipsing the central role of African nationalism, he embraced what emerged as the nonracial and collaborative work of the ANC with the SAIC and SACP and he joined their various protests and boycotts. In 1943, Mandela joined the ANC Youth League (ANCYL), and from that time until his death, his life and work were inextricably tied to the party and its mission to forge a free and democratic South Africa, and in 1947, he was elected to the ANC executive of the Transvaal.

THE STRUGGLE

By the early 1950s, an Afrikaner (descendant of the first White Dutch-speaking settlers who colonized parts of South Africa from the mid seventeenth century) dominated government and established all-encompassing policy of apartheid, a deeply racist philosophy that entrenched White supremacy and Black oppression. By then, Mandela was fully committed to the "struggle," a broad movement by Blacks to reverse apartheid and establish a nonracial democracy. Over the course of the next few years, he reluctantly sacrificed family life and his marriage to his first wife Evelyn Mase, whom he had met in Johannesburg through the Sisulus, for the cause. He had also, in 1953, established with future president of the ANC, Oliver Tambo, the law firm of Mandela and Tambo to serve Africans, especially those confronted by apartheid laws. By then, the Afrikaner-dominated National Party (NP) had come to power and articulated its dreaded policy of apartheid. Mandela was elected, in 1951, as chair of the ANCYL, which was an incubator for more radical leaders. In response, Mandela engaged fully in the work of the Congress of the People and in developing the Freedom Charter, the guiding document of the ANC that stipulated demands for full democracy and economic opportunity. He moreover took the same personal risk as thousands of South Africans to openly challenge the apartheid government and its racist laws in the Defiance Campaign of 1952. These were the watershed years for most opposition political leaders in South Africa for the government made it clear it would brook no open challenge to its policies or authority to enforce them with a brutal hand. Mandela and 155 other members of various opposition parties were confronted by the full effect of the new laws, including the sweeping Suppression of Communism Act of 1950. This law made virtually any public act or commentary directed at changing or reforming apartheid tantamount to "communism" and therefore subjected the perpetrator to prosecution. Mandela and his fellow defiance campaigners were thus tried in the infamous Treason Trial of 1952 for, among other things, their mass protests against the hated pass laws that subjected Blacks but not Whites to strictly documented movement in and out of Whites-only areas of the country.

Once marked by the trial, Mandela and others were condemned to a life of harassment by state security, repeated jail time, and banning orders that prevented them from freedom of association and political expression. In response, Mandela proposed the implementation of his M-Plan (M for Mandela) which laid out a structure the ANC to operate underground with clandestine cell groups should it be banned as was the SACP. In 1958, following his divorce from Evelyn, he married Winnie Madikizela, a woman who would, in many controversial ways, also become central to his political work.

As the government escalated its control of Black lives to serve White interests during the 1950s, Mandela and his colleagues were confronted by an invidious choice as to whether to maintain the ANC's central principle of engaging only in nonviolent protest. Then, on March 21, 1960, state police fired on unarmed protestors in the notorious Sharpeville massacre, killing 69 people and wounding 180 others. Mandela felt that since the state made it clear it was prepared to use violence to enforce its policies and White supremacy and so had already dictated the terms of engagement, the ANC had no choice but to adopt the armed struggle. In a fateful decision, Mandela and others, including Walter Sisulu and Joe Slovo, established Umkhonto We Sizwe (The Spear of the Nation, known as MK) as the armed wing of the ANC. MK's mission was to commit acts of sabotage against government installations, not human or "soft targets," to compel the state to enter into negotiations for a new democratic constitution. In order to facilitate the development of MK and avoid police scrutiny, Mandela went underground as David Motsamyi, driver for Cecil Williams, a White member of the allied Congress of Delegates. The ANC High Command then directed Mandela to leave the country secretly on a tour of Africa to raise funds and to train in military weapons and tactics and sabotage. Under the pretense of attending a Pan African Freedom Movement for East Central and Southern Africa conference in Addis Ababa, Ethiopia in February of 1962, Mandela left South Africa and traveled through Botswana to Tanzania,

Ethiopia, Morocco, and a number of West African countries before making a short detour to London, England where he met with Oliver Tambo, who was living in exile following the Treason Trial. While on the trip, not only did he raise significant funds and commitments for training support from a number of African leaders, he also underwent in Ethiopia a few months of rigorous military training himself.

PRISON

It was not long after his return to South Africa in August of 1962 that Mandela was picked up by police to face what was the defining experience of his life, his twenty-seven years in prison. Following a five-year sentence for political agitation and for leaving the country without permission, Mandela was implicated, while in jail, for his role in Operation Mayibuye and his work with MK, both of which were aimed, so the state claimed, at the violent overthrow of the government. The ensuing Rivonia Trial, named for the area where police raided an ANC hideout that harbored a number of ANC, SACP, and MK leaders, revealed Mandela's work with the newly developed armed struggle. It was while in the dock at that trial that Mandela made his impassioned "I am prepared to die speech" (see appendix B), a testament to his commitment to work for a free and democratic South Africa. Despite the real fear of a death sentence, Mandela and his coaccused remained stoically defiant and so committed to each other that none of them would accept any plea bargain to mitigate sentencing. In the end, the life sentence was, many felt, tantamount to death for it extinguished any possibility of a personal or political life outside prison, or so the state thought.

Mandela's long years of incarceration—eighteen of them in the notorious Robben Island Prison set out in Table Bay, within sight of majestic Cape Town but otherwise hopelessly out of reach—were in unexpected ways both the making and unmaking of the man. They certainly were the unmaking of a man who could maintain any semblance of a normal life. He was cut off from family, including his politically active wife Winnie, friends, and

his work. He moreover suffered many hardships both physical and emotional. He and fellow political prisoners were subjected to hard labor in the lime quarry on Robben Island where sun reflecting off the white lime seared their eyes and skin. The food and cells were often of subhuman standard, and the International Red Cross was compelled to intervene on numerous occasions. More significantly, he was unable to communicate with the outside world, or be quoted or seen. Indeed, he virtually disappeared from the world's gaze, and most people could only guess at what he looked like after a few years, though his image would later be popularized as the iconic symbol of the global antiapartheid movement. Paradoxically, however, the state and prison services could not diminish his spirit. Mandela used his time in prison to significant effect. He and others referred to the work in collaborative educational discussions as "the university," and he was able to win over many concessions for more humane treatment through his polite but determined lobbying and shaming of prison guards and officials. He and fellow inmates such as Ahmed Kathrada, Mac Maharaj, and Walter Sisulu were also able to further hone ANC policy and planning while in jail. His important and widely read autobiography was also drafted and smuggled out of Robben Island.

Mandela's tireless commitment to the struggle and his resolve not to allow prison to break him persisted over the years as the apartheid state weakened. The combined effects of global isolation as a pariah state, sanctions, and especially mass opposition and boycotts in South Africa were starting to bite. Nelson Mandela, or at least his image and reputation as a key African leader, provided the rallying point for change, and the government was forced to pay attention to him. In 1982, he was transferred to the mainland Pollsmoor Prison and then to a cottage at the more comfortable Victor Verster Prison as prelude to his release.

FREEDOM AND THE PRESIDENCY

On February 11, 1990, Nelson Mandela emerged from twenty-seven years in prison clearly older and bruised but otherwise undiminished in his life-long commitment to bring about a free and democratic South Africa. Despite being in his seventies and having endured nearly three decades in prison, there was no opportunity, and apparently no desire on his part, to just sit back and enjoy his freedom. There were, however, many tumultuous times ahead. F. W. de Klerk's NP government had conceded the need for change, but remained suspicious of the ANC and more ominously, wedded to maintaining safeguards for White privilege. Additionally, other political organizations, including reactionary Whites on the far right and radical African nationalists threatened to plunge the country into violent chaos. Others, including the regionally powerful Inkatha Freedom Party under Mangosuthu Buthelezi, demanded special dispensations to safeguard their sectarian interests. There are too many twists in the story to cover here, but suffice it to say, it was nothing short of miraculous that Mandela was able to shepherd the parties through to a negotiated settlement. His patient understanding and respect for all parties was the key to success. Despite the profound challenges of violence perpetrated by the shadowy "third force" of the old White government, Mandela counseled patience. Through the implementation of the Truth and Reconciliation Commission in 1996, he showed the nation that forgiveness and inclusion would be vital for the survival of the fragile new democracy. Such was his success that he and F. W. de Klerk were recognized with the shared Nobel Peace Prize in 1990.

As president from 1994–1999, Nelson Mandela demonstrated a heroic level of patience and understanding that surpassed expectations. He deftly navigated a shared government of national unity that provided reassurances to the White minority that they still had a place in South Africa, and he presided over the development of what is revered as one of the world's most progressive constitutions with specific safeguards for women to be included in the structures of government. There remain, however, many grave challenges to the fulfilment of many of the aspirational goals for housing land redistribution, health care, and education, among others. Significantly, he also refused to run for a second term, despite widespread calls to do so. He wanted to ensure that South African democracy did not run the risk of devolving into despotic rule as some African nations such as Zimbabwe suffered. Thanks to Nelson Mandela, South Africa enjoyed a relatively smooth process of transition to full democracy and free and fair democratic elections are still, more or less, the rule despite the obvious challenges created by the corruption of Jacob Zuma's presidency.

PERSONAL LIFE AND LEGACY

Nelson Mandela was mindful of his iconic role as president and world leader though it left little room for his personal life. Following his release from prison, he faced a number of personal challenges that took a toll. First, his wife Winnie, who had served as proxy for him in the popular imagination, became increasingly problematic. Although he still professed his love for her, Winnie's antics and criminality became a personal and political liability. Her corruption, an affair, and especially her complicity in violent criminal acts compelled Mandela to divorce Winnie even if he could not publicly disavow her. He also made many efforts to save the reputation of the ANC and its leaders from accusations of corruption, but not always successfully. The gifts of cash he made to Jacob Zuma did nothing to help him avoid staggering graft when he became president. Some, including Archbishop Desmond Tutu, criticized Mandela and others in the ANC for self-indulgent and profligate ways while the country suffered from rampant unemployment and poverty. The AIDS epidemic in South Africa also revealed cracks in the presidential edifice. Mandela was widely condemned for his refusal to grapple with the public health calamity and allowing Thabo Mbeki, who emerged as an AIDS denialist, to succeed him. It took the very painful personal tragedy of Mandela's son Makgahto dying from an AIDS-related illness to spur him to take a public stance promoting AIDS awareness in a country that deeply stigmatized the disease.

Despite a few other love interests, it was not until Mandela united with Graca Machel, the widow of Samora Machel, the former president of Mozambique, that he again seemed to find marital happiness. On his retirement from the presidency, Mandela continued to serve as a global leader in some capacities, particularly through the Elders group of former statesmen. He wisely stayed out of party politics, at least publicly, so he could concentrate on the important historical legacy he has left with the Nelson Mandela Foundation. His passing on December 5, 2013, led to worldwide grieving and acclamation for what many see as his heroic life. His iconic, smiling face, however, has become a worldwide symbol of courage and the fight for human rights. Indeed, across South Africa, his name appears on streets and avenues, buildings and public parks, and events of celebration too numerous to list here. His image, moreover, appears on everything from boxes of South Africa's signature Rooibos herbal tea to the country's currency, postage stamps of many other nations, posters, T-shirts, and more. His association with "Brand South Africa" has perhaps become too exploited for some, but it is hard to imagine it without him.

Entries A–Z

A

AFRICAN NATIONAL CONGRESS FOUN-DATIONS 1912–1939. The African National Congress (ANC), which Nelson Mandela joined in April of 1944 and later became president of in 1991, had its origins in the early twentieth century among leading political and Western-educated intellectual African men. First established as the South African Native National Congress (SANNC) in 1912 and later, in 1923, renamed the ANC to affirm its African nationalist priorities, it is among the oldest national liberation political movements in the world. Over the course of its history, the ANC drew from a wide range of political and economic ideologies and withstood many challenges to emerge as the paramount political party by the 1990s. In 1994, under the leadership of Mandela, it won an overwhelming majority with over 62 percent of the popular vote in the nation's first-ever inclusive democratic elections. The ANC then took the leading role in a transitional **Government of National Unity** (GNU) with Mandela as president and shared power with the two other leading parties, the National Party (NP) and the Inkatha Freedom Party (IFP). It has remained the dominant political party in leadership to the present, though it has faced many challenges from across the political spectrum.

Among the key early influences that shaped the ANC were Christian mission education and the outgrowth of African independent churches; an emergent vibrant African press; and tentative alliances with other African, Indian, Coloured (an official term referring to people of mixed-race descent in

apartheid South Africa), and working-class political movements. Rural African chiefs who represented significant links to a heritage of long-standing resistance and opposition to White domination dating back to the eighteenth century also shaped the organization. These combined impetuses tended to support the leaders following a conservative or *hamba kahle* (isiZulu for "to go safely") political approach that included passive resistance, deputations, and petitioning the British colonial and local South African White governments. In its formative years, the ANC sought to represent African concerns about limits to their economic opportunities and their ill-treatment by Whites. Following the South African War (1899–1901), the planned formation of a White-dominated Union of South Africa in 1910 meant the extension and expansion of colonial laws and practices aimed at segregating and exploiting Africans across the country. In 1909, Pixley Kalsaka Seme (1881–1951), a lawyer from Natal Province, and Solomon Tshekisho Plaatje (1876–1932), a journalist and writer from the Orange Free State, called for Africans from across the country to set aside past differences and meet in Bloemfontein to form the South African Native Convention (SANC) and to formulate responses to the challenges posed by the impending formation of the Union government.

By 1912, in response to increasing pressures from the White-dominated Union government, the SANC expanded to include chiefs from rural areas, Christian and mission-educated Africans, as well as African elites. Under the leadership of the Revd. John Langalibele Dube (1871–1946), a mission-educated celebrated writer, newspaper editor, and politician, Seme and Plaatje along with Saul Msane (d. 1919) and James Tshangana (J. T.) Gumede (1867–1946), formed the ANC with Dube serving as the founding president. Among the first concerns of Congress were the Union's legislation aimed at limiting educated Africans' rights to vote and their rights of residence and to purchase land. In the Cape Province, some educated Africans and Coloureds had retained the right to vote under an ostensibly color-blind franchise. Among the most repressive and limiting pieces of legislation was the 1913 Natives Land Act, which aimed to end African rent tenancies on White land, and more problematically, to circumscribe African rights to the land. The 1913 Act set aside over 90 percent of the land in the country for exclusive White ownership and relegated Africans to just 7 percent in a series of fragmented reserves (the figure were later adjusted to 87 percent for Whites and 13 percent for Africans). In a calculated effort to divide and rule Africans, the reserves were designated along ethnic lines and administered by White government officials through the local authority of approved or appointed chiefs. As part of a wider set of policies aimed at dealing with the "Native Question," the Union government coupled this land legislation with increased taxation on Africans, constraints on wages and unionizing, and banning strike activity. As Africans faced more economic hardship, greater pressure to migrate to White-owned farms and urban and mining areas in search of wage-labor, and decreasing opportunities to participate in government, their resistance and protests intensified. The ANC led the way with peaceful petitioning and, in 1914 and again in 1919, sent delegations to the United Kingdom to protest the outcomes of the Act of Union and especially the 1913 Land Act. The ANC's efforts were largely in vain as British authorities rebuffed deputation to London, and the Union government increased pressures on Black (a term which includes Africans, Coloureds, and Indians) working-class people in response to growing labor unrest.

By the 1920s, the ANC faced internal political challenges as the influence of international socialism and communism took root among Africans, Indians, and White radicals, and the organization began to stall. While the ANC leadership focused primarily on reforming the 1913 Land Act and on voting rights, issues that were of greater interest to elite Africans than to common workers, it lost traction with wider grassroots popular concerns and resistance. Across the country, working-class men and women struggling with state repression more openly confronted the White government with protests and resistance. Among the more pernicious laws that Africans challenged were the much-hated "pass laws," legislation that compelled Blacks to carry identity documents or passes that established their legal place of residence in the reserves and outlined limited rights to be in "White areas." Africans were further radicalized by the effects of repressive labor laws that both strictly limited their rights to organize and strike while also ensuring they could not ally with White workers. As White communists and labor organizers courted Africans in support of a wider nonracial opposition to the government, the ANC faced new challenges for the makeup and direction of the organization. From 1921, the newly established Communist Party of South Africa (CPSA, later reformed as the South African Communist Party, or SACP) emerged as the only officially nonracial political organization and recruited among mostly urban African workers, while in the countryside, the Industrial and Commercial Workers Union (ICU) attracted aspirant Black farmers. Although many in the ANC affirmed the principle of nonracialism, in 1923, the leadership prioritized its African nationalist identity over concerns about the growing influence of White trade unionists with an internationalist outlook. African communists such as Moses Kotane, nevertheless, started to join the ANC as dual members in a practice that would lead to greater integration of the two parties. In 1927, J. T. Gumede was elected president and sought to embrace the more radical political forces emerging at the time. The membership ousted him in

1930, however, and the ANC became moribund, losing even more political ground over the next few years as it clung to a conservative reformist approach while the majority of Blacks engaged in more direct action with public protests, strikes, and boycotts.

As the pall of depression and fascism spread across the world, the ANC sought to broaden its base. In 1935, the president Pixley Ka Isaka Seme led the ANC to the **All Africa Convention** (AAC) where Black leaders from across the country met to strategize about how to resist even more deeply racist and segregationist legislation set out by the Afrikaner prime minister Barry Hertzog. Still heavily influenced by conservative chiefs whose positions increasingly relied on government approval, the AAC and ANC got few concessions from the White government and ultimately accepted the 1936 institution of a "Native Representative Council" (NRC). Intended ostensibly to serve as a conduit for African interests to the White state, the NRC functioned as a hollow talking-shop and ANC participation further eroded its credibility in the eyes of the majority of Africans.

AFRICAN NATIONAL CONGRESS AND MANDELA, 1940–1950. From the 1940s, the African National Congress (ANC) had to contend with the rising tides of rapidly expanding African participation in urbanization and wage labor as it sought to broaden its base and form alliances with other oppressed groups in the country. As more Africans—men and women—poured into the urban and industrial areas of the country in search of wage labor to meet tax demands and to purchase consumer goods, the state struggled to implement a coherent set of policies to meet the demands of the White-dominated political economy. Africans became increasingly frustrated with the local and national governments' capricious application of pass laws and the dizzying array of laws and regulations aimed at constraining their movement in the "White Areas" of the country. Even under the new leadership of Alfred Xuma as president, the party still seemed to primarily follow rather than lead the growing grassroots opposition to state oppres-

sion and segregation legislation. When Anton Lembede, president of the ANC from 1943 until his sudden death from a heart attack in 1947, and others, sought to connect the ANC to radical mass-action campaigns including squatters' protests, bus boycotts over price hikes, and protests against the pass laws, the ANC leadership was compelled to adapt. The ANC became more open to working with communists and, for the first time at the 1943 party conference, women were allowed to join as members in their own right. It was in 1942 that the ambitious, young lawyer-in-training Nelson Mandela took notice of these political developments and joined the ANC.

Mandela was among the vanguard of young men who challenged the old guard of the ANC to embrace the more radical and popular forms of resistance that would drive the party. In 1944, Mandela joined with **Oliver Tambo** and **Walter Sisulu** under the leadership of Lembede to form the ANC Youth League (ANCYL). In their manifesto, the ANCYL outlined what they saw as the key elements necessary to effect change in South Africa. These included eschewing the previous methods of moderation and passive petitioning of the government for change. It also condemned the old guard of the party for representing primarily middle-class liberal values and for seeking their own class interests, prepared as they were to accept meagre offerings from the White minority government on behalf of the Black majority. It further rejected the current dispensations of unequal access to land and resources as well as the principle of "trusteeship" whereby paternalist Whites in government would determine the slow process of "civilizing" Blacks. They called for Black self-determination and the end to racial oppression.

By1946, the ANC began to more openly support other major opposition movements, and in particular the South African Indian Congress (SAIC) and their very effective mass-action passive-resistance campaign. It was during this period that the ANC wrestled with questions and challenges related to the political and philosophical ideology of their movement. One powerful wing of the ANCYL, led by Lembede, emphasized the African nationalist ideology of the organization. Early on, Lembede made a deep impression on Mandela, and he embraced the exclusive Africanist philosophy. For Lembede and others who would later develop this ideology into the Pan African Congress (PAC) and Black Consciousness Movement, collaboration with Whites and communists was anathema to the self-determination outlined in the Programme of Action and the African nationalist essence of the ANC. In it, they argued that the liberation struggle in South Africa was more about racism than class conflict. In the event, by the 1940s, there was significant overlap in the membership of both the ANCYL and the CPSA (later SACP) as well as a strong sense that the struggle was about both institutionalized racism and the exploitation of workers; the intersection of race and class oppression. Mandela, Sisulu, and Tambo, who had worked closely with the communists (and Mandela would even join the SACP) started to recognize that the ANC must work with others, including the SAIC as well as communists and trade unionists to create a broad front of opposition. Additionally, following the death of Anton Lembede in 1947, those who supported a nonracial basis for change and democracy gained the upper hand. The rise to power of Daniel François Malan's National Party (NP) in the Whites-only apartheid election of 1948 was a defining moment of the conflict in South Africa. This victory provided a mandate for Malan (prime minister from 1948–1954) and his party to consolidate and extend White supremacist power in law and the economy over and against the Black majority. Moreover it empowered Afrikaners as an ethnic bloc in government and state-run enterprises while simultaneously criminalizing almost all forms of opposition. Particularly vexing to the ANC as well as Indian and Coloured people were Malan's early apartheid laws such as the Population Registration Act, the Group Areas Act, and the Separate Registration of Voters bill that aimed to divide, dilute, and exclude Black voters from participation in the Whites-only democratic government. Equally pernicious was the sweeping

Suppression of Communism Act that, in the context of the unfolding Cold War, characterized virtually any opposition to the state and apartheid as illegal. In response, in 1949, the ANCYL, favoring a broad nonracial platform, elected James Moroka, who affirmed both more active resistance and collaboration other opposition groups president. Mandela, Sisulu, and Tambo were also elected to the national executive, setting the stage for a more radical approach over the next decade.

AFRICAN NATIONAL CONGRESS AND MANDELA, 1950–1970. Through the 1950s, the African National Congress (ANC) developed new tactics and strategies and Nelson Mandela played a key role in shaping the policies. He abandoned his previous dogmatic views that the ANC should work exclusively as an Africanist organization and slowly recognized the need to collaborate, and he affirmed the use of strikes, boycotts, stay-at-homes, and various forms of civil disobedience to undermine apartheid. In 1952, in alliance with the South African Indian Congress (SAIC) and the Franchise Action Committee, the ANC set in motion the **Defiance Campaign** in which over ten thousand supporters defied apartheid laws and courted arrest and imprisonment, vowing not to accept bail or fines as punishment. The government charged Mandela, along with the ANC president, James Moroka, **Walter Sisulu**, and others with fomenting a revolt. Mandela and Sisulu were convicted of "statutory communism" and received suspended sentences of nine months hard labor while some other young offenders were whipped or jailed. By the end of the campaign, over eight thousand resistors had been jailed, fined or beaten. Thus, began the state's criminalization of Black protest politics and resistance. In anticipation of even further repression and the likelihood that the ANC would be banned as the CPSA was, in 1953 Mandela devised a new strategy to allow the organization to continue to operate. The M-Plan (M for Mandela) laid out a comprehensive organizational structure that would allow the ANC to operate underground within the country. Although the key leadership and operations would, by the 1960s, be directed by leaders in exile such as **Oliver Tambo**, the M-Plan remained a key internal part of the opposition movement's approach that anticipated Mandela playing a key role, though this would later be frustrated by his imprisonment.

A more broad front was then developed in 1955 when the ANC led the vanguard of the Congress Alliance of opposition parties to Kliptown, outside of **Johannesburg** where over four hundred delegates met on June 25 in a **Congress of the People**. They represented a multiracial alliance of Black (the ANC), White (the Congress of Democrats [COD]), Indian (SAIC), and Coloured (the Coloured People's Congress [CPC]) political organizations as well as the multiracial South African Congress of Trade Unions (SACTU), where they adopted the **Freedom Charter**. The central guiding clause of the charter, which would later form the cornerstone of a postapartheid constitution, was the statement that the South Africa belongs to all who live in it, Black and White, and that no government can justly claim authority unless it is based on the will of all the people. The charter, moreover, stated that all people should be treated equally before the law, and that all those who worked should share in the land and wealth of the country. In response to the country-wide escalation of resistance, the government, in 1956, arrested 156 members of the opposition, including Nelson Mandela and most leading members of the ANC, erstwhile CPSA, and others for treason. The infamous **Treason Trial** dragged on until 1961, all the while striking fear among African political leaders and their families while also hampering the efforts of the ANC to organize and effectively oppose the state. By the end of the decade, The ANC had, nevertheless, gained worldwide recognition for its efforts to fight apartheid, and for the work of Nkosi (chief) **Albert Luthuli**, ANC president from 1952–1967, who was awarded the Nobel Peace Prize in 1960.

The 1960s were a watershed decade for Mandela and the ANC. Most leaders were compelled to either go underground and operate clandestinely, as with Mandela and Sisulu—at least until their arrest and life sentence, or go into exile. Meanwhile, many African nationalists questioned the ANC's commitment to nonracial policies and the inclusion of White communists in the protest movement. In 1959, Robert Sobukwe led a significant faction to break away and form the Pan African Congress (PAC), which focused on exclusively Black African efforts at opposition and competed with the ANC for popular support. A greater crisis emerged in 1960 after ANC president Luthuli announced a campaign to defy the pernicious pass laws that required every African to carry documentation of permission to work or live in vast areas of the country reserved for Whites. Robert Sobukwe and the PAC preempted the ANC and launched its own antipass campaign on March 21, 1960. On that day, in the Black township of Sharpeville, police opened fire on unarmed protestors, killing sixty-nine and wounding nearly two hundred others in what became known as the Sharpeville Massacre. Following the massacre and other widespread violent and brutal government repression of Black resistance, Nelson Mandela and other ANC leaders made the fateful decision to abandon the policy of nonviolence. Arguing that it was the violent, oppressive state that had dictated the terms of the conflict, Mandela proposed the ANC form a military wing **Umkhonto We Sizwe (MK, the Spear of the Nation)**, with him as commander, to carry out acts of sabotage against the government. On December 16, 1960, MK began a bombing campaign against government buildings and infrastructure. In the wake of all the widespread resistance, the government also banned both the ANC and the PAC, preventing them from organizing or operating openly. This drove the remaining ANC leadership, such as Oliver and **Adelaide Tambo**, either underground or into exile until the 1990s. Those leaders who remained in the open, or were captured as was Mandela, were banned and imprisoned, cutting them off from all political activities as well as family and friends.

Perhaps the biggest blow to the ANC was the state security apparatus effective infiltration of the organization leading to the **Rivonia Trial** and the imprisonment of many leaders of the ANC. By this time Mandela, as head of MK, had convinced key members of the leadership to undertake the use of violence and the armed struggle. Emanating from this was a mostly aspirational and unrealistic plan known as Operation Mayibuye ("Bring back Africa"). The planning document for this operation was among the papers police found at Liliesleaf Farm in Rivonia and which formed a key element in the prosecution of ANC leaders in the trial. By the end of the trial, key members of the ANC and CPSA were jailed for life, including Mandela who was arrested later on a tip from an American informant.

Over the next two decades, the ANC was severely hampered by government repression. The South African government declared the ANC a terrorist organization and members either in prison or subject to arrest. With the leadership either in prison or in exile, the organization was unable to organize or openly challenge the apartheid state. Following Luthuli's leadership, the next president, Oliver Tambo, operated in exile and worked on cultivating worldwide opposition to the South African state with the global antiapartheid movement. Nelson Mandela and other ANC and opposition leaders imprisoned on Robben Island, such as **Ahmad Kathrada**, **Mac Maharaj**, Raymond Mahlaba, **Walter Sisulu**, and **Govan Mbeki**, nevertheless continued to plan for their eventual release and liberation of the country. At their major conference in 1969, held in exile in Morogoro, Tanzania, the ANC openly embraced support from the Soviet Union, established a revolutionary council including president Tambo, and communists **Yusuf Dadoo** and **Joe Slovo** and officially opened its membership to Whites. Mass opposition to the apartheid government continued, moreover, to spread internally across the country, led by new generations of leaders and especially the township youth that supported the outlawed ANC. Among their most well-known actions was the June 16, 1976 student protest march and planned boycott against the government's implementation of mandatory instruction equally in both Afrikaans and English for all Black schools. Over ten thousand high-school students stayed away from school that day and took to streets in Soweto in defiance of the new law. The government responded to the Soweto uprising with brutal repression. State police fired on the unarmed students killing at least 175 and wounding perhaps over 1,000. The atrocity, especially the now famous photo of Mbuyisa Makhubo carrying the limp body of twelve-year-old child Hector Pieterson who had been shot by police, drew international opprobrium and brought into wider recognition the work of the ANC and their calls for support of the global antiapartheid movement.

AFRICAN NATIONAL CONGRESS AND MANDELA, 1970–1990. Over the next ten years, further uprisings and resistance were met with increasing levels of state violence and repression. The South African liberation struggle was also caught up in the wider continental tensions between left-leaning or communist-aligned new African nations and regimes backed by anticommunist Western states such as the United States and Great Britain. Indeed, the African National Congress's (ANC) use of violence in various acts of sabotage against the regime during this period were part of the wider "armed struggle" orchestrated by MK and for which, in addition to South Africa government, the United States and Great Britain labelled the organization and its leaders, including Nelson Mandela, "terrorists." The acts, which lasted from 1979 to 1983, included bombings of courts, police stations, restaurants, an oil refinery, and the Koeberg nuclear power plant, and which left numerous civilians as well as White police and military personnel dead or wounded. Over fifty bombings and acts of sabotage were planned carried out by members of MK, who operated from or were supported by ANC bases outside the country. By the 1980s, the ANC operated from multiple African countries, ranging from frontline states such as Botswana, Zimbabwe (led from 1980 by an African majority government after a protracted resistance war), and Mozambique, to more distant training bases in Angola, Tanzania, and Zambia as well as form central offices in London.

In response to the escalation of armed conflict and the perceived threat of socialist states in the region, the South African NP government under **Pieter Willem (P. W.) Botha** developed a "total strategy" against those seeking to topple the regime that included both a "hearts and minds" component and military operations. The impressive and powerful South African Defense Force (SADF) as well as various proxy armies engaged in an all-out offensive against ANC personnel and bases across Africa as well as supporting counterrevolutionary forces in Angola, Mozambique, and Zimbabwe. Ruth First, wife of **Joe Slovo** and a Communist Party ally of the ANC, and Dulcie September, an ANC representative working in Paris, were both killed by South African agents, the former by a parcel bomb sent to her in exile in Mozambique, the latter in 1988 by an assassin. The pressure on many frontline states, as well as the SADF wars of counterinsurgency throughout the region, was too great for some to withstand. Mozambique, for example, was compelled to sign the Nkomati Accord in 1984. The accord outlined an agreement whereby Mozambique would stop supporting ANC bases in its country while the South Africans undertook to stop supporting the Mozambique National Resistance movement against the ruling Mozambique Liberation Front government. These and other dimensions of the total strategy significantly undermined the ANC's operations and support across the African continent.

Following Botha's disastrous implementation of a new constitution that excluded the African majority in 1983, the ANC then pivoted toward intensifying mass action within South Africa. In a clandestine address on the ANC's Radio Freedom, **Oliver Tambo** called on all South Africans to boycott the upcoming elections for the new parliament that allowed only Whites, Indians, and Coloureds to vote for separate houses. Moreover, he reaffirmed the call for everyone to work to make the country ungovernable in order to undermine National Party (NP) rule. In response, Botha instituted a series of states of emergency to allow for an even greater clampdown on opposition activities. At this point, the broad-based vanguard of opposition reformed under the auspices of the United Democratic Front (UDF). Representing a wide range of organizations such as student groups, churches, trade unions, and

civic associations, the UDF espoused most of the ANC's aims, but it officially eschewed the use of violence, preferring mass passive resistance. Simultaneously, international opprobrium against the South African government intensified and even former stalwart Cold War allies of the regime such as Ronald Reagan and Margaret Thatcher finally joined in leveling a wide range of sanctions against the country. In a controversial move, however, some younger ANC supporters in the townships, known as "comrades," undertook their own forms of vigilante justice. These included kangaroo courts and the infamous practice of "necklacing" where comrades killed informants or traitors by hanging gasoline-soaked car tires around their necks and setting them alight. **Winnie-Madikizela-Mandela**'s public advocacy of this practice as well as troubling reports of the torture, abuse, and murder of ANC trainees in camps outside the country were perhaps the nadir of ANC practices through the 1980s. The ANC, with only partial success, tried to restore its leadership in the country with the initially failed Operation Vula, which was intended to secrete exiled leaders into South Africa across the border from various frontline states. From 1986 through 1990, ANC and SACP operatives, including **Mac Maharaj** and Ronnie Kasrils, head of military intelligence for MK, infiltrated back into the country. The discovery of Operation Vula by the government in 1990, however, significantly jeopardized the efforts to plan for a negotiated end to apartheid. There were, however, other avenues for negotiations. In 1985, leading White South African businessmen started to make their own overtures to the ANC in an effort to bring the country back from the brink of violence and the concomitant downward economic spiral that had already gripped the country. Gavin Reilly of the Anglo-American corporation, which had vast interests in mining and manufacturing, and other scions of White business met with Oliver, then still in exile, in Zambia to discuss a way forward.

Following repressive state restrictions on the activities of the UDF in 1989, mass action was headed by the more loosely defined Mass Democratic Movement (MDM). The Congress of South African Trade Unions (COSATU), a member of the alliance with the still-banned ANC and SACP, took the lead in the MDM, pressing for the worldwide intensification of economic and political sanctions against the South African government. At the same time, international efforts to ratchet up sanctions and the isolation of the White-minority government were starting to take a toll on the NP's government. A vital part of these pressures was the public relations campaign to remediate the image of the ANC and its leadership from being seen as terrorists to being understood as political prisoners and victims of systematic racism. At the center of this effort was the image of Nelson Mandela who, though not having been seen in public for over twenty-five years, became the symbolic hero of the cause, celebrated in the Free Nelson Mandela campaign.

The prelude to proper negotiations with the ANC was the back-channel efforts at talks about talks, which centered on Mandela. As domestic and international pressure mounted during the 1980s, the NP government had sought a way out. Beginning in 1982, Botha authorized the transfer of Mandela and several other ANC leaders from Robben Island to Pollsmoor Prison on the mainland in Cape Town. This was done in part to appease the antiapartheid movement, which saw the island as a place notorious for poor conditions, isolation, and hard labor. The move was also made to facilitate talks as well as to potentially acclimate Mandela to a life outside prison and possibly to remove Mandela's influence on the new generation of ANC leaders, who were by that time also serving sentences on Robben Island. In 1985, Botha then called on Mandela and the ANC to renounce violence and the armed struggle as a precondition for negotiations and offered him freedom if he would do so. In a powerfully worded rebuke, read out by his daughter **Zindzi Mandela** (Mandela himself could still not speak publicly), Mandela rejected the offer, noting that it had been the NP which had historically used violence to repress the opposition. He stated that there could be no negotiations unless and until opposition parties and leaders, including himself and the ANC, were unbanned and freed. Once in Pollsmoor Prison, Mandela did, nevertheless, begin opening channels to NP government officials to open the way for talks. In 1986, he met with Hendrik "Kobie" Coetsee, minister of justice, to further communications at a time when the government seemed open to some sort of negotiated settlement. It was these discussions that Mandela would later be harshly criticized for, especially by ANC hardliners who were still incarcerated on Robben Island. They felt he had acted unilaterally and without proper consultation with the party leadership and had also possible "sold out" in a bid to become leader. In 1988, Mandela was diagnosed with tuberculosis, no doubt a consequence of his long years in prison, and his ill health threatened to derail discussions about negotiations. After treatment and recovery in Tygerberg hospital and Constantia Medical Center, he was moved to the more salubrious Victor Verster Prison farm near Paarl, outside Cape Town, where he was given the use of a former warden's house and garden as part of the preparations for his eventual release. Mandela did hold a brief, secret meeting with Botha to discuss how to plan for negotiations, but he still insisted that the ANC and its leaders must be set free first, and that they would not accept any preconditions.

AFRICAN NATIONAL CONGRESS AND MANDELA, 1990–2013. The African National Congress's (ANC) success after long decades of struggle started to became apparent once the National Party (NP) government conceded that it could no longer avoid negotiating with the most popular political force in the country. Following the repressive rule of President **P. W. Botha**, who in the event had suffered a debilitating stroke and had also lost the confidence of his party to manage the country, **Fredrik Willem de Klerk** assumed the leadership of the party and the country. A more enlightened and realistic politician than his predecessors, de Klerk understood his role as facilitating a transition to a negotiated settlement with the ANC. He hoped he could somehow preserve minority blocks of White power and privilege within a sort of federal, decentralized state that would dilute ANC political domination while also avoiding an outright violent conflagration. Nelson Mandela met with de Klerk in December 1989. The following February, de Klerk announced in parliament that the ANC and other opposition parties would be unbanned. A few days later, on February 11, 1990, Mandela was released from Victor Verster and welcomed by a largely elated and relieved nation.

The next four years were a roller coaster of tension and conflict as the ANC negotiated its way to an all democratic election, and its victory. By September of 1990, MK had agreed to suspend the armed struggle while de Klerk's NP government, still technically in power, agreed to the gradual release of all political prisoners. In 1991, the ANC agreed to sign a National Peace Accord, along with other opposition parties, including the South African Communist Party (SACP) and the Congress of South African Trade Unions (COSATU), the Pan African Congress (PAC), as well as various White political parties such as the NP and Afrikaner parties, in which they renounced violence and committed to negotiations for a fully democratic country. Then, in 1992, for the last time, the NP government held an all-Whites referendum to seek a mandate to negotiate and nearly 70 percent of Whites supported moving ahead. This set the stage for the protracted and challenging Convention for a Democratic South Africa (CODESA).

Representatives at CODESA struggled through often bitter and contested negotiations that were marred by dirty tricks and the government's persistent efforts to destabilize the process. These included a secret yet state-sponsored "third force" which aimed to support desperate efforts by **Mangosuthu Buthelezi** and the Inkatha Freedom Party (IFP) to use violence against ANC supporters. Despite Mandela's best efforts and remarkable statesmanship, the violence spread and other opposition organizations rejected the NP government's bid to ensure it had a guarantee for power-sharing and protections for minority rights in a new government. Through shrewd diplomacy, **Cyril Ramaphosa** (current president of South Africa) and Mandela along with Roelf Myer of the NP steered the parties back

to the table to finalize an agreement for elections and a constituent assembly.

On April 27, 1994 (now a national holiday in the country), all South Africans were able to participate in the country's first fully democratic election based on nonracial universal suffrage in a unitary parliamentary system. The ANC won a significant majority with 62 percent of the vote, and filling 252 of the 400 parliamentary seats, though this was less than the two-thirds majority needed to unilaterally amend a new constitution. Mandela, president of the ANC since 1992, was elected by the National Assembly as the first Black president of the new South Africa. According to the interim agreement, Mandela was compelled by the constitution and the two-thirds rule to share power in a **Government of National Unity** (GNU). This included the two parties with next largest number of seats, the NP and IFP, and de Klerk representing the NP served as one deputy president alongside the ANC's **Thabo Mbeki**. **Mangosuthu Buthelezi**, representing the IFP, headed up the important post of minister of home affairs, and IFP members were invited to join Mandela's cabinet. The GNU, however, also ensured continued tensions and conflicts as Mandela and the ANC was faced with ongoing efforts by these two parties to destabilize the country in a vain attempt to grab power through regional divisions and decentralization. Despite the challenges of the GNU, and that de Klerk and the NP withdrew from it in 1996, it did serve to stabilize the new nation and to work toward reconciliation.

A signal achievement of the GNU was the acclaimed, though still controversial, Truth and Reconciliation Commission (TRC), established in 1996, and still in operation. The TRC took evidence of politically motivated crimes from thousands of witnesses and perpetrators in a process of restorative justice, and offered amnesty to all who confessed fully and acknowledged their crime. While principally intended to address crimes committed against the majority Black population opponents of apartheid, almost all of which had never been fully investigated, the TRC also called on members of the ANC and other opposition parties to make confessions. In a controversial action, the ANC rejected accepting any responsibility for having perpetrated crimes including bombings in the country and acts committed against those accused of being traitors or informants in the townships or in their training camps in exile.

In 1999, the GNU expired and the ANC won the next election, again with a sweeping majority, taking over 66 percent of the vote—this time, however, without Nelson Mandela as leader. Mandela stepped down, in part because by then, as an octogenarian, he was perhaps feeling the physical strains of leadership, but also to ensure the road to full democracy could be followed without falling into the trap of a leadership cult that had plagued many other new African democracies. He gave way, not to who many predicted would be his heir apparent, the accomplished trade unionist, Cyril Ramaphosa, but rather to Thabo Mbeki. Mbeki, a party stalwart and bookish, was a controversial figure, not least because of his

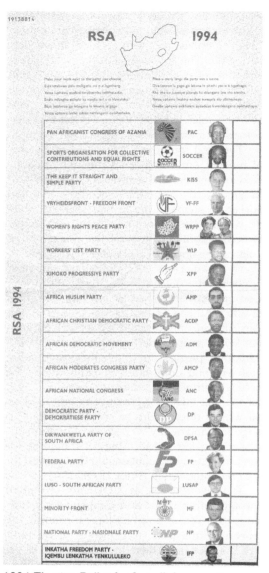

Portrait of Nelson Mandela, 2001. *Courtesy of Jurgen Schadeberg.*

1994 Election Ballot for first all democratic election. Nelson Mandela is 12 down from the top. *Courtesy of Aran MacKinnon.*

ill-informed and often bizarre response to the **HIV/AIDS** crisis that was overwhelming the country and Mandela's family.

Since the turn of the twenty-first century, the ANC has held on to power despite many controversies and scandals. Thabo Mbeki resigned in his second term as president owing to internal dissent, leaving the post to

Kgalema Motlanthe as custodian for a year. **Jacob Zuma**, the flamboyant populist leader from Zululand, served two terms as a deeply personally flawed and corrupt leader. Mandela died before the end of Zuma's second term, and many felt the ANC had indeed lost its guiding light and succumbed to the sort of unethical one-party state rule that plagued other new African democracies. Accordingly, the ANC also suffered a steady ebbing of support in the popular vote as new and established parties on both the right and left gained ground. Many criticized the ANC for its failure to deliver on its mandate and commitment to an improved economy (South Africa was among the most economically unequal countries in the world), employment opportunities, equitable land redistribution away from Whites who still own a disproportionate amount of the land, as well as improved education and health care for all. It is yet to be seen whether the current president, Cyril Ramaphosa, can steer the party and its government back to solid foundation.

AFRICA TOUR 1962. See MANDELA'S AFRICA TOUR 1962.

ALEXANDRA TOWNSHIP. After leaving the rural Transkei in his youth, Nelson Mandela's first point of arrival in Johannesburg, the largest urban area and gold-mining center of South Africa, was Alexandra Township, or "Alex." Planned by and named after the wife of the White farmer who owned the land in 1912, the township was originally intended for White settlement, but owing to its distance of about eight miles from the city center few moved there and it was designated for Africans. Significantly, having been established prior to the 1913 Natives Land Act, Africans could legally purchase and own land freehold in Alexandra until the 1930s when segregationist legislation prohibited it. While he always thought of Alex as his first home in the city, it was also where Mandela first experienced the grinding poverty and blight of the Black townships where migrant workers from the countryside struggled to find decent jobs and wages. He rented a room from the Reverend Mabutho at 46 Eighth Avenue amidst the vibrant, often boisterous streets of the area, where electricity outages were common and sanitary facilities were few. In order to save on bus fares, Mandela often walked a twelve-mile round trip from Alex to work the law offices of **Lazar Sidelsky**'s law firm. Mandela and other residents, however, remembered the area with affection as an exciting center where Zulu, **Xhosa**, Sotho, Pedi, and other ethnicities shared music, culture, and life.

ALL AFRICA CONVENTION. Over four hundred African representatives from across the region of Southern Africa gathered in Bloemfontein, the site of the establishment of the **African National Congress** (ANC) in 1912, to coordinate their efforts in articulating and supporting their rights and opposition to segregation and later apartheid laws in the All Africa Convention (AAC). On December 16, 1935, Professor Davidson Don Tengo (D. D. T.) Jabavu, and ANC President Prixley kalsaka Seme, led the assembled delegates in affirming their grievances over the loss of voting rights and access to land under new legislation enacted by the all-White government of Prime Minister Barry Hertzog. Thereafter, the delegates agreed to petition the government for redress of their largely educated, African middle-class interests and to meet every three years to further their aims. When their deputations and petitioning were repeatedly rebuffed by the government, the AAC steadily lost credibility and popularity. Due to Jabavu's agreement, after 1936, to work with government's newly formed Native Representative Councils, which provided for African interests to be shared with the government by a White official and without any direct democratic involvement, many younger radicals started to leave the AAC. By the 1940s, a new generation of ANC supporters such as James Moroka overwhelmed the old guard of the AAC and their efforts to maintain unity in the convention. By 1950, the AAC was moribund, eclipsed by the more radical vanguard of Nelson Mandela's generation and the ANC Youth League.

B

BENSON, MARY (December 8, 1919–June 19, 2000). Originally from a middle-class, White South African family of Anglo-Irish descent that accepted the status quo of segregation, Mary Benson became a civil rights advocate and early chronicler of the **African National Congress** (ANC) and the liberation struggle, as well as a friend and biographer to Nelson Mandela. From an early age, Benson sought a career in theater and films, though this led her from America to the United Kingdom where she eventually worked with the South African Women's Army contingent during World War II and then as an assistant to the celebrated film director David Lean. Following the war, she returned to South Africa where her reading of Alan Paton's famous novel, *Cry the Beloved Country* (1948), inspired her to take an interest in the plight of Black South Africans and their struggle against racism and apartheid. While in London, she became acquainted with the Reverend Michael Scott, a British missionary who was, at the time, championing the cause of the Herero and Nama of Namibia (then Southwest Africa) who were fighting against incorporation into what was to become a South African–administered mandate territory. Scott was, in 1946, credited with being the first White to be jailed for opposing the country's racist laws. Benson worked with Scott in London and then in South Africa helping establish the African Bureau, which aimed to support Africans in need of legal defense against racist laws. It was through this work that by the 1950s, Benson became acquainted with Nelson Man-

dela. When Mandela and others were charged and tried in the **Treason Trial**, Benson offered her considerable organizational and writing skills to the defense team of the accused and assisted in publicizing their plight. Her work with the antiapartheid movement continued, and in June 1961, she was in London to help host Nelson Mandela while he was on his clandestine trip across Africa, and briefly to Britain, to raise funds and undertake military training. Following her return to South Africa, Benson wrote for various newspapers about those fighting apartheid. She was, moreover, among the first South Africans to testify before the United Nations Special Committee Against Apartheid in 1963. Her work drew the attention of the government, and as with so many others who opposed apartheid, she too was banned in 1964. She later fled, again to London, where she began working on various biographies and histories of the struggle, including *Chief Albert Luthuli of South Africa, African Patriots: The Story of the African National Congress of South Africa*. These and others dating back to the 1960s were among the earliest researched works on the Black people and organizations involved in the antiapartheid struggle. Indeed, her acclaimed 1986 biography, *Nelson Mandela: The Man and the Movement*, based on a series of clandestine personal interviews with Mandela while he was underground prior to his arrest and twenty-seven-year imprisonment, was the first. Mandela remained in touch with Benson after his release and election to the presidency, even visiting her in 2000 just a few months before she passed away.

BERNSTEIN, LIONEL "RUSTY" (March 20, 1920–June 23, 2002). "Rusty" Bernstein, the son of European Jewish immigrants to South Africa, was an antiapartheid activist and central figure in the South African Communist Party (SACP, formerly the Communist Party of South Africa [CPSA]), which he and his wife, Hilda Bernstein (née Schwarz) joined in the late 1930s. After serving as an artillery gunner for Britain in World War II, Bernstein returned to South Africa and worked supporting various labor union actions and organizations. Both he and Hilda were charged with sedition in 1946 for their role in supporting the widescale mineworkers strike with public relations publications. Bernstein went on to be the long-serving editor of *Fighting Talk*, the official journal of the SACP. He then played a key leadership role in **Congress of Democrats** (COD) and helped forge its collaborations with the **African National Congress** (ANC). It was through this relationship that Bernstein met Nelson Mandela and other ANC leaders. In 1954, he helped organize the national **Congress of the People** that drew together the ANC, COD, and the South African Indian Congress (SAIC) to protest various apartheid legislation. Indeed, it was Bernstein's gift for writing that enabled him to draft many of the now-iconic phrases of the **Freedom Charter**, which became the guiding document of the liberation struggle. What followed was the tragically familiar harassment by the state, and repeated banning orders and censorship of his and Hilda's writing. In 1955–1956, the state charged and tried Bernstein, Hilda, and 153 others with treason. Ultimately acquitted, Bernstein continued to work underground with the SACP and ANC, including with the planning group that drafted proposals for Operation Mayibuye, which aimed to destabilize the government and country through mass action and sabotage. On July 11, 1963, he and eighteen others were arrested at Liliesleaf Farm, the secret location where leading members of **Umkhonto We Sizwe (MK)** and the SACP, including **Walter Sisulu**, **Govan Mbeki**, Raymond Mhlaba, **Ahmed Kathrada**, and Bob Hepple, who were working on planning operations. Bernstein and twelve others, including Nelson Mandela, who was not at Liliesleaf but was in jail at the time, were brought to the infamous **Rivonia Trial**. Bernstein was one of the few defendants acquitted on charges at the trial, and was let out on bail after being rearrested. He and his wife Hilda then fled South Africa and made their way through Botswana and Zambia and eventually to the United Kingdom, where their children eventually joined them. Bernstein continued to serve the ANC by later teaching at the organization's Solomon Mhlangu Freedom College for exiles in Tanzania. The Bernsteins returned to South Africa in 1994 after the first all-democratic election, and he served briefly as a press office for the ANC before passing away in 2002.

BIZOS, GEORGE (November 14, 1928–). A human-rights lawyer, friend, and personal counsel to Nelson Mandela, George Bizos was part of the legal team, along with **Joel Joffe**, **Bram Fischer**, Vernon Berrange, and Arthur Chaskalson, that defended Mandela and others at the **Rivonia Trial** and was instrumental in assisting the defendants in escaping the death penalty. Bizos arrived in South Africa with his father in 1941 from Greece as a refugee from World War II. After earning his law degree at the University of the Witwatersrand, he was called to the South African Bar in 1954. He then embarked on a distinguished career as a defense attorney and fighting for human rights during the apartheid era. Among his more famous clients, in addition to Mandela, were other antiapartheid political activists such as **Denis Goldberg**, **Mac Maharaj**, **Walter Sisulu**, Steve Biko's family, and, in more than twenty cases, **Winnie Madikizela-Mandela**. Bizos also made important representations for victims at the Truth and Reconciliation Commission (TRC). Mandela and the **African National Congress** (ANC) leadership later called on Bizos to assist in drafting a new constitution for South Africa, a document that is recognized for its progressive nature and protection of human rights. In 1999, then-President Mandela awarded Bizos the Order for Meritorious Service Class II medal and, in 2004, the International Bar Association recognized him with the prestigious Bernard Simons Memorial Award.

BOTHA, PIETER WILLEM (January 12, 1916–October 31, 2006). The sixth state president of South Africa from 1978–1989, "P. W." Botha presided over perhaps the most tumultuous period of the apartheid era. Known for his intransigent White supremacist views and unwavering support for Afrikaners and the National Party (NP), "P. W." was also referred to as the "*die groot krokodil*" (Afrikaans for the "great crocodile," a reference to his emotionless indifference to protests and Black self-determination) who had been a Nazi sympathizer during World War II. He escalated the entrenchment of segregation in the country through widespread forced removals of Blacks from "White areas." A staunch Cold War critic of what he perceived as widespread Soviet-sponsored communism in and beyond South Africa, Botha formulated a "total strategy" to combat African insurgency in the country and in neighboring states and to garner support from similarly minded Western leaders such as President Ronald Reagan and Prime Minister Margaret Thatcher. Such strategies enabled Botha to resist demands for democratic reform and the growing international movement to free Nelson Mandela from prison. Mounting pressures nevertheless compelled Botha to institute some reforms and in 1983 he drafted a new constitution that at once made him state president (consolidating the powers previously held by a prime minister and a president as symbolic head of state) and laid out a disastrous reimagining of apartheid. Under the new constitution, Whites, Indians (South Asians), and Coloureds were provided seats in tricameral parliament with disproportionate power remaining in White hands. Africans were excluded entirely from the government to be administered within their own fragmented, economically depressed, and woefully inadequate areas referred to as "Bantustans" (also known as "homelands"). It was, in large measure, this "reform" that sparked the **African National Congress** (ANC) and its proxy United Democratic Front (UDF) move to make the townships ungovernable and to escalate mass protests across the country. Facing escalating violence and a downward spiral of the economy driven by international sanctions against the country, Botha eased some features of "petty" social apartheid laws such as segregated facilities and the prohibition of marriage across racial lines. Botha, however, refused to conciliate or negotiate with the ANC until his actions and attacks on ANC operatives in frontline states drew censure from the United States. Facing further isolation from the growing global antiapartheid movement, Botha made overtures to Nelson Mandela, offering him release from prison if he would renounce the armed struggle. Mandela refused and Botha retreated into an even more insular posture by enforcing almost continuous states of emergency which crippled the country. The combination of international censure for South Africa's military interventions in Angola, Mozambique, and other frontline states with a stroke and failing health forced Botha to resign in 1989, giving way to the presidency of **Frederik Willem de Klerk** and the transition to a democratic South Africa. At the time of Botha's death in 2006, Mandela made a conciliatory statement noting some of the attempts he had at reforming apartheid, though the Truth and Reconciliation Commission (TRC) charged him with gross violations of human rights.

BUTHELEZI, MANGOSUTH "GATSHA" (August 27 1928–). Mangosuthu Buthelezi, leader of the powerful, regionally based, ethnic-nationalist Inkatha Freedom Party (IFP) he founded in support of separatist ambitions, served as minister of home affairs under Nelson Mandela's presidency. Descended from a past king of the Zulu people, Dinzulu kaCetshwayo (1868–1013), who led an independent state in the northeast of South Africa that lasted from 1816 until conquest in 1879, Buthelezi also served Chief Minister of the KwaZulu homeland or "Bantustan" during apartheid. A shrewd politician who occasionally engaged in dangerous brinksmanship, Buthelezi could be confrontational and often supported using violent tactics and protests as he built his regional powerbase as a counterpoise to the **African National Congress** (ANC). In his early life, Buthelezi followed many of the same pathways that Mandela had. Following schooling at Adams College in KwaZulu Natal, a mission school affiliated with the United Congregational Church of Southern Africa, Buthelezi went on to the **University of Fort Hare** to study history and Bantu administration. Similar to Mandela's experience, Buthelezi was expelled from Fort Hare in 1950 for joining a protest against an official visit by the Governor General, though he later completed his degree through the University of Natal. While at Fort Hare, Buthelezi learned about the ANC and protest politics from the likes of professor Z. K. Matthews and the later leader of the Pan African Congress (PAC), Robert Sobukwe. Buthelezi joined the ANC and supported its opposition to apartheid and institutional racism in South Africa. Buthelezi, however, embarked on a different path than the ANC when he revived the Zulu cultural movement known as Inkatha (literally a grass coil that symbolized the unity of the Zulu kingdom) and fashioned it into an ethnic nationalist party based in KwaZulu-Natal. In the 1970s, Buthelezi walked the tightrope of working with the White government through the Bantu Authorities administration, which many in the ANC and opposition saw as a collaboration with apartheid. He accepted appointment as the chief executive officer of the KwaZulu Territorial Authority, and along with this, financial and political dependence on the apartheid state. Although he rejected full "independence" for KwaZulu as a separate "homeland" under the reforms offered by President **Pieter Willem Botha**, Buthelezi nevertheless pursued a separatist stance in support of a reinvented Zulu traditionalism. In so doing, he rejected the primacy of the ANC and its platform of fighting for a single, unitary state that the ANC would indubitably dominate. In the late 1980s, as the country reached the tipping point between some sort of democratic change or a spiral into mass action and potential civil war, Buthelezi stepped up his efforts to secure his ethnic-nationalist power base. In what is widely acknowledged as a collaboration with a secretive "third force" later revealed to have been run by the state-sponsored Civil Cooperation Bureau, Buthelezi was seen to be complicit, along with President **Frederik Willem de Klerk**, in facilitating widespread violence, especially in and around the mining compounds of **Johannesburg**. Elements of the IFP who brandished both "traditional" Zulu weapons such as spears and shields along with conventional weapons were seen to have been aided by South African state police as they infiltrated and attacked ANC strongholds in Black urban areas. Despite passionate entreaties by Nelson Mandela in a joint statement with Buthelezi to both Inkatha supporters and ANC "comrades" who had retaliated to throw their weapons into the sea and end the violence, the conflict continued through negotiations to end apartheid and right up to the eve of the first democratic elections in 1994. Indeed, Buthelezi initially refused to participate in the elections, a posture calculated to derail the transition and likely to provoke even more intense violence across the country. He demanded a guaranteed constitutional safeguard for the Zulu monarchy and land in trust to support the Zulu nation and this challenged the ANC's plan for a unitary state. It was only at the eleventh hour, and through the intervention of an international team of mediators, including Henry Kissinger, former U.S. secretary of state under Richard Nixon, that Buthelezi agreed to enter the elections, thus requiring his picture to be added by hand to hundreds of thousands of ballots already printed. Recognizing the volatility of the fragile new democracy in 1994, President Mandela appointed Buthelezi into his cabinet as minister of home affairs, a post he served in for a second term under President **Thabo Mbeki**. As a further gesture of reconciliation, Mandela also appointed Buthelezi to serve as acting president on some occasions when he was out of the country on official business. Although the IFP lost support across the country thanks to the rising popularity of future ANC President **Jacob Zuma** and because of Buthelezi's increasingly sectarian ethnic politics, he remained a powerful regional force until his retirement from politics in August of 2019.

CACHALIA, AMINA (June 28, 1930–January 31, 2013). An antiapartheid activist and leader in the South African women's movement, Amina Cachalia (née Asvat) grew up in the South Asian community of the Transvaal (now Gauteng Province) among dedicated civil rights opponents of segregation and apartheid. Her father, Ebrahim Ismail Asvat, had worked closely with Mohandas Gandhi on his passive-resistance campaign. After her father passed away when she was twelve, Amina was strongly influenced by members of the South African Communist Party (SACP) and she joined the Transvaal Indian Youth Congress which was, by the 1950s, working to establish an alliance with the **African National Congress** (ANC). Along with her later-to-be husband **Yusuf Cachalia**, she then met and befriended Nelson Mandela and they helped organize and publicize the **Defiance Campaign** in 1952. Frustrated by the government's refusal to issue her a passport so she could study in India, she turned to working with other women leaders to establish the South African Federation of Women and she played a leading role in the organization's efforts to protest oppressive laws against women. Following her work in support of those accused during the **Treason Trial** in the 1950s, Amina was targeted for scrutiny by state security forces. By 1963, she was served with the first of a series of banning orders. These eventually overlapped with banning orders of her activist husband, Yusuf, and in a bizarre feature of life in apartheid South Africa, the two were forced to apply for special permission to be able to

speak to each as banned people within a marriage. Despite her banning, she was able to assist in the planning of the escape of Arthur Goldreich, Harold Wolpe, and others from jail after their prosecution during the **Rivonia Trial**. She later became active in the United Democratic Front (UDF) and its efforts at mass resistance leading to the all-democratic elections in 1994, when she won a seat in parliament as a member of the ANC. She and Mandela shared a close friendship. Mandela recalled an occasion prior to his imprisonment where the two prepared a pigeon pie and Amina and her husband Yusuf were among the few political allies that the state allowed to visit Mandela when he was still in prison in 1988. Mandela apparently reserved a special fondness for Amina. Though she declined, he proposed marriage to her after Yusuf passed away in 1995 and Mandela was separated from his second wife, **Winnie Madikizela-Mandela**. In 2004, The ANC government awarded her the Order of Luthuli in Bronze for her commitment to the antiapartheid struggle and support of women's rights.

CACHALIA, MAULVI ISMAIL (December 5, 1908–August 8, 2003). A South African–born South Asian from the Transvaal (now Gauteng Province), Mauvli Cachalia was a leading member of the South African Indian Congress (SAIC) who collaborated extensively with the **African National Congress** (ANC). Cachalia's father, Ahmed Mohamed Cachalia, had been jailed for his work with Mohandas Gandhi's passive-resistance campaign from 1907–1914. Mauvli was a central figure in the

South African Indian passive-resistance campaign in 1946. He then turned to working more directly with the ANC and efforts to opposed apartheid as did his brother, **Yusuf Cachalia**. In 1952, he was appointed deputy volunteer chief to Nelson Mandela, who was then volunteer chief for the **Defiance Campaign**. By the mid-1950s, Maulvi Cachalia had been officially banned by the state and was forced to operate clandestinely in his work with **Chief Albert Luthuli** and Mandela on proposals to develop a plan of armed resistance, which culminated in the formation of **Umkhonto We Sizwe (MK)**. Despite his banning order, he secretly left the country to attend the anticolonial Asian-African Conference in Bandung, Indonesia in 1955 as a delegate for the SAIC and ANC. The antiimperialist World Peace Council also presented him an award that same year. After the Sharpeville Massacre of 1960, Cachalia was arrested, among thousands of others, under a state of emergency targeting members of the Congress Alliance of the SAIC and the ANC in opposition to apartheid. By 1966, he had fled South Africa and established an office of the ANC in New Delhi, India. He divided his time between India and South Africa until 1990, when following the unbanning of the ANC, he returned to South Africa to witness the first all-democratic elections in 1994.

CACHALIA, YUSUF (January 15, 1915–April 10, 1995). Younger brother to Mauvli Ismail Cachalia, Yusuf Cachalia was a stalwart member of the Transvaal and South African Indian Congresses (SAIC) and worked for close cooperation between the SAIC and the **African National Congress** (ANC). He was among the SAIC leaders who helped forge the Congress Alliance and worked with ANC leaders on the **Defiance Campaign**. Cachalia had one unfortunate run-in with Nelson Mandela in the early 1950s, when as an ANC Youth League member, Mandela was adamantly opposed to collaboration with outside groups. This included opposing the "foreign influenced" communists and the SAIC that some members of the Youth League felt were trying to upstage the ANC. The then-somewhat-mercurial Mandela was so hostile to these organizations, he even

pushed Cachalia off the stage as he attempted to deliver a speech in support of ANC collaboration with the SAIC-led passive resistance campaign. The two later developed a friendship and supportive working relationship. Indeed, Yusuf and his second (he was, for a time, married to Bette du Toit, and Afrikaner trade unionist) wife **Amina Cachalia** were among the few members of the opposition movement who, after repeated entreaties to the state, were able to visit Mandela while he was still in jail at Pollsmoor Prison. Both Yusuf and his wife Amina suffered banning orders from the government for much of their married life that prohibited them from meeting with any other banned person. In the bizarre world of apartheid South Africa, the married couple were then compelled to apply to the government for special permission to speak to each other. Mandela attended his funeral in 1995 and remained close with Amina and the family after Yusuf's passing. Mandela later reportedly proposed marriage to Amina, though she declined.

CANAAN BAPTIST CHURCH. On his first visit to the United States as president of the new South Africa, Nelson Mandela visited Canaan Baptist Church in Harlem, New York. Among those in the audience and congregation at the historic African American church he addressed after the Sunday service on were former Mayor David Dinkins, Congressional Representative Charles Rangle, the Rev. Jesse Jackson, civil rights advocate Al Sharpton, singer Roberta Flack, and boxing promoter Don King. Mandela was on a diplomatic mission to address the United Nations and the United States Congress, and to seek investment in the newly democratic South Africa. Canaan Baptist Church had long been involved in the antiapartheid struggle.

CLARKEBURY BOARDING INSTITUTE HIGH SCHOOL. This was Nelson Mandela's first formal Christian Western educational institution. Established in 1830 as part of the Clarkebury Wesleyan Methodist Society Mission village and named after the Wesleyan theologian Dr. Adam Clarke, Clarkebury School at Ngcobo

President of South Africa, Nelson Mandela with members of the Congressional Black Caucus including Representative Kweisi Mfume. *Courtesy of the Library of Congress.*

in the Transkei was near to Mandela's childhood home of Qunu, and, at that time, one of the largest schools for Africans in the region. Following some primary education at the church school at **Mqhekezweni, "the Great Place,"** Mandela's guardian, **Chief Jongitaba Dalindyebo**, also a graduate of the Clarkebury School, sent him there in 1934, as he did his son **Justice**. Chief Dalindyebo felt that, in addition to education in African history, culture, customs, and politics, Mandela would need skills based on Western educational programs in order to serve as an effective councilor to the king as his father Henry Gadla Mandela had done. The headmaster at Clarkebury, Reverend Cecil Harris, introduced Mandela to a staunchly British imperial worldview as well as to a love of gardening. In 1937, after two years of study, Mandela earned his junior certificate at Clarkebury, the equivalent to completing a junior year in an American high school, and was ready to move on the **Healdtown School** to complete his high-school education.

COLLINS, LEWIS JOHN (March 23, 1905– December 31, 1982). Appointed as Canon of St. Paul's Cathedral in London in 1948, John Collins was an Anglican priest who took an abiding interest in human-rights causes and especially the plight of Black South Africans. Educated at Cambridge University and a champion of various social movements including the Campaign for Nuclear Disarmament and Christian Action and the British Anti-Apartheid Movement, a charitable organization that funded various causes for victims of conflict, Collins first visited South Africa in 1954 to witness the devastating effects of the migrant labor economy and exploitation of African workers under the system of apartheid. While there he met with Nelson Mandela, **Oliver Tambo, Walter Sisulu**, and **Chief Albert Luthuli**, the then-president of the ANC. Two years later, at the behest of the Archbishop of **Johannesburg**, Ambrose Reeves, Collins raised over £75,000 in the United Kingdom to help with the costs of defending Mandela and others at the **Treason Trial**. Thereafter, Collins established the Defence and Aid Fund to channel funds for legal aid to South Africans during the apartheid era. He further extended his support to those fighting apartheid by establishing in 1981 the Canon Collins Educational Trust for Southern Africa to support education for refugees from South Africa and Namibia exiled in Britain.

CONGRESS OF DEMOCRATS. Formed in 1953 by left-wing antiapartheid Whites and at the urging of leading members of the **African National Congress** (ANC), the South African Indian Congress (SAIC), the Congress of South African Trade Unions (COSATU), and the South African Coloured People's Organization (SACPO), the Congress of Democrats (COD) served to more directly connect White liberal South Africans to the nonracial struggle for equality and democracy. Following the growing momentum of the **Defiance Campaign**, which Nelson Mandela had been instrumental in organizing, and in the wake of the banning of the South African Communist Party (SACP), a range of communists as well as leading White opponents of apartheid including **Lionel "Rusty" Bernstein**, **Cecil Williams**, **Bram Fischer**, **Joe Slovo**, **Ruth First**, and **Helen Joseph**, formed the COD and forged an alliance with Black antiapartheid organizations in the Congress Alliance to publicize the ANC political platform. In such a sharply segregated society, and a context where White radical labor unionists and communists did not see eye to eye with African nationalists over opposition politics, ANC membership was not yet open to Whites and few had joined the ANC prior to the 1970s. Although the ANC was committed to a nonracial society—as opposed to the Pan African Congress (PAC), which took a firm Black nationalist stance—the organization felt it needed to promote its cause among sympathetic Whites by taking the lead in an alliance between White and Black organizations. The COD remained active despite its relatively small membership until 1962 when it was banned by the South African state.

CONGRESS OF THE PEOPLE AND THE FREEDOM CHARTER. The Congress of the People on June 26, 1955, the brainchild of Professor Zachariah Matthews, president of the **African National Congress** (ANC) in the Cape region, was an effort by antiapartheid groups to organize and coordinate their philosophy and strategies. As opposition to the new apartheid government broadened and gathered strength in the 1950s, state repression made it increasingly difficult for antiapartheid leaders and parties to organize. Consequently, the ANC had lost some of its momentum and Professor Matthews believed a mass meeting would reinvigorate action. Crucially, the congress was also to be the place that opposition parties gathered to formulate and approve the **Freedom Charter**, which would become the defining document for the ANC and ultimately a new postapartheid constitution. After a year of planning, over three thousand delegates from across the country met at Kliptown, near **Johannesburg**, to ratify the charter and to plan future actions and collaborations. Among the leading organizations that sent delegates were the ANC, the South African Congress of Trade Unions (SACTU), the South African Indian Congress (SAIC), the all-White **Congress of Democrats** (COD), and the recently formed Coloured People's Congress (CPC). The government had outlawed the South African Communist Party (SACP) in 1950, and prior to its reformulation, it could only send delegates under the auspices of other organizations such as SACTU. At the congress meeting, the assembled representative adopted the Freedom Charter (see appendix A), which had been drafted previously by leading members of the ANC and the SACP, including **Lionel "Rusty" Bernstein**. It was this document, and the structures of party governance developed at the congress, that served as the foundations of the ANC and the postapartheid constitution.

D

DADOO, DR. YUSUF (September 5, 1909–September 19, 1983). The son of Gujarati Indians who immigrated to South Africa in the 1880s, Yusuf Dadoo opposed race and class oppression from an early age. Dadoo was influenced by nationalists who had challenged the British in India and by the experience of his father, Mohammad, who had once been successfully defended in court by the famous Indian nationalist and spiritual leader Mohandas Gandhi against a racially based eviction notice. Following early education in South Africa and India, Dadoo completed his medical degree at the prestigious University of Edinburgh. It was in the United Kingdom that Dadoo cultivated his political ideals among Labour Party and communist leaders. On his return to South Africa, he played leading roles in the Transvaal Indian Congress and the Communist Party ([CPSA], and the re-formed South African Communist Party [SACP] from 1953). Dadoo first came to Nelson Mandela's notice in the 1940s when, as president of the Transvaal Indian Congress, Dadoo worked successfully with another medical doctor, Dr. Gangathura Naicker, president of the Natal Indian Congress, to orchestrate a country-wide Indian *Satyagraha* passive-resistance campaign. Mandela was much impressed with Dadoo and Naicker's leadership when, following Jan Smuts' government's promulgation of the 1946 Asiatic Land Tenure Act (Pegging Act) that severely limited and oppressed Indians' freedom of movement, as well as land and business ownership, they led thousands to openly defy the state and court

arrest in protest. **African National Congress** (ANC) leaders took note of the success of the passive-resistance campaign's tactic of open mass defiance of the state on moral grounds. As an Indian and a committed communist, Dadoo also played an important role in softening Mandela's views on collaboration with Indian opponents of apartheid as well as his participation in the Communist Party. He also played an important role in inspiring younger generations of Indians to follow the communist strategy and take up the struggle against apartheid. Notable among them was **Ahmed Kathrada**, a **Rivonia Trial** defendant and fellow Robben Island prisoner with Mandela. Dadoo and Mandela became close friends and allies and worked closely together on the **Defiance Campaign**. Following the Suppression of Communism Act, which provided the government with a wide-ranging interpretation of communism as virtually any opposition to the apartheid state, and the Sharpeville Massacre, Dadoo went into exile in the United Kingdom to avoid arrest. Mandela met again with Dadoo in London in 1962 during his training tour outside South Africa. It was in that meeting that Mandela laid out a plan to enhance the Black African nationalist image of the ANC despite Dadoo's entreaties to maintain the appearance of broad nonracial coalition. Dadoo, nevertheless, remained loyal to Mandela and supportive of the new ANC approach. Following visits to the Union of Soviet Socialist Republics, Dadoo became a well-known antiapartheid lobbyist, making fiery speeches at the United Nations in 1964, and, later that year, accepting the Joliot Curie Gold Medal for Peace from the Algerian Peace Committee and Algeria's President, Houari Souyah, on behalf of Mandela, who was, by then, in prison. Dadoo remained an active SACP leader and representative in Europe and across Africa until his death in 1983, and he was buried near Karl Marx's grave in Highgate Cemetery, London.

DALINDYEBO, NKOSI (CHIEF) JONGI-TABA DAVID (c. 1900–August 19, 1942). Nkosi Jongitaba Dalindyebo served as regent paramount chief of the **Thembu** royal house from 1928 to 1942, and as Nelson Mandela's guardian and mentor following his father, **Henry Gadla Mandela**'s death in 1930. It was at the chief's **Mqhekezweni, "the Great Place,"** that Mandela met the chief's wife, Inkosozana (princess) NoEngland Dalindyebo, who cared for Nelson as a mother, and his son **Justice Dalindyebo**, whom he befriended and would later travel to college and **Johannesburg** with. As a devout Wesleyan and traditional chief, a not uncommon combination among African leaders, Jongitaba taught Mandela about Methodism Thembu African leadership, history, and culture. It was in the chief's household that Mandela came of age as a young man, undergoing the customary circumcision ritual of *abakhwetha* and earning a new additional name, Dalibunga, meaning "leader of the council." It was also from Jongitaba Dalindyebo's guardianship that Nelson and Justice fled to Johannesburg to escape marriages arranged by the chief. The chief represented many of Mandela's ties to "traditional" and customary rural African culture and politics, and these were resources that he drew upon throughout his life.

DALINYEBO, NKOSI JUSTICE MAMBIL-ANG MTIRARA (1914–1974; exact dates unknown). The son of the regent paramount **Chief Jongitaba Dalindyebo**, Justice befriended Nelson Mandela as brother on his arrival at **Mqhekezweni, "the Great Place,"** in 1930. The two young men shared many experiences, including the circumcision ritual, and, following traditional protocols, Mandela was intended to serve as councilor to Justice, just

as his father, **Henry Gadla**, had served as a royal councilor. Both Justice and Nelson were also to be subjected to unwelcome arranged marriages by chief Dalindyebo. Following his involvement in controversial student protests at the **University of Fort Hare**, which drew the ire of the chief, Nelson devised to abscond from the Transkei and join Justice in search of a job and excitement in the mining city of **Johannesburg**. Once there, Justice enlisted the aid of an uncle, Mpondombinni, to get both the young men jobs on the mines until Mandela embarked on his law career. Thereafter, he and Mandela parted ways as Justice returned home after the passing of his father, Chief Jongintaba, and married Makhulu Nozolile, whom his father had earlier chosen for him. After his release from prison, Mandela had a brick house built for Makhulu, Justice's widow and the last surviving member of the family that had cared for him at Mqhekezweni, "the Great Place," as a token of appreciation for her family had done for him.

DEFIANCE CAMPAIGN. Following the apartheid election of 1948 and the Verwoerd government's implementation of even more restrictive racist and discriminatory legislation, the **African National Congress** (ANC), under the driving force of a new generation of ANC Youth League leaders such as Nelson Mandela, **Walter Sisulu**, and **Oliver Tambo**, set in motion the Defiance Campaign for June 26, 1952, in accordance with the ANC's adoption of a more confrontational approach to protest politics outlined in the Programme of Action. This included extending the sorts of passive resistance and noncooperation that was the hallmark of earlier actions by Mohandas Gandhi and the South African Indian Congress (SAIC) to rolling mass action and civil disobedience with boycotts, strikes, and stayaways. Indeed, the stated purpose of the campaign was to defy unjust apartheid laws by courting arrest by, among other acts, breaking curfews for Blacks, for using "Whites only" public amenities, and by Indians seeking to enter townships designated for Africans only. In a break with the more exclusive African nationalist practices of the past, Mandela and Sisulu arranged for the ANC to collaborate with the SAIC on the campaign, including working with Indian leaders **Yusuf Dadoo** and **Ismail Cachalia** on a national executive board. The state security police reacted swiftly and with brutality. Mandela and Cachalia were arrested on the first day of the campaign ostensibly for breaking curfew, but as with all the others, they were charged with violating the sweeping Suppression of Communism Act even though they had intended to avoid arrest by acting as observers. Other ANC and SAIC leaders were arrested in the following days for "statutory communism." Police use of force, including shooting, and arrests only served to spread the campaign across the country like wildfire and the planned nonviolent approach gave way to some riots in areas where protestors had been whipped or killed. From a few hundred arrests in June, the campaign provoked over eight thousand arrests by the end of the year, clogging the jails and courts as anticipated. Most of those arrested were ultimately released with only a fine or short sentence. Major leaders such as

Mandela, Sisulu, Dadoo, and Cachalia, among others, however, were also later charged in 1956 with high treason in the infamous **Treason Trial** for acts dating back to the Defiance Campaign in 1952. By 1953, **Chief Albert Luthuli**, then-president of the ANC, called for the campaign to be suspended in the face of the state's use of violence and the need to reconsider tactics. Overall, the ANC claimed the campaign a success in terms of mobilizing mass protest action across the country and gaining worldwide recognition for its opposition to apartheid. It also paved the way for future collaborative campaigns under the Congress Alliance and a more militant approach to opposing the apartheid government.

DE KLERK, FREDERIK WILLEM (March 19, 1936–). The seventh state president of South Africa, Frederik Willem—better known as "F. W." de Klerk, was the key transitional leader of the apartheid government who was responsible for having Nelson Mandela released from prison

F. W. de Klerk, left, the last president of apartheid-era South Africa, and Nelson Mandela, his successor, wait to speak in Philadelphia, Pennsylvania. *Courtesy of the Library of Congress.*

and was also instrumental in the process of negotiating a settlement that led to the **African National Congress** (ANC) taking power in 1994. Significantly, de Klerk shared the 1993 Nobel Peace Prize with Mandela, awarded for their role in ending apartheid. De Klerk hailed from a prominent Afrikaner political family, and followed a traditional path into political leadership in the dominant majority Afrikaner National Party (NP). His father, Johannes "Jan" de Klerk, had served in various cabinet ministerial posts during the 1950s and 1960s, including as minister of home affairs, a post that F. W. later held, and briefly for nine days as state president in 1975. F. W.'s older brother, Willem, was an academic and journalist who eschewed NP politics that supported apartheid and so helped establish the liberal Democratic Party in the Whites-only parliamentary system prior to the end of apartheid. Following studies in law at the University of Potchefstroom, where he met his first wife, Marike (née Willemse), he embarked on a successful law career and was about to join the ranks of academe when called upon by leaders in the NP to stand for an open seat in parliament. He rose rapidly through the ranks of party politics, and was revered by party members as a staunch conservative supporter of the party line and apartheid. Under the presidency of **Pieter Willem (P. W.) Botha**, de Klerk was appointed to various ministerial positions in the cabinet of President Botha, including Minister of Post and Telecommunications and Sport and Recreation (1978–1979); Mines, Energy and Environmental Planning (1979–1980); Mineral and Energy Affairs (1980–1982); Internal Affairs (1982–1985); and National Education and Planning (1984–1989). Following a stroke and lack of support for his political intransigence over apartheid policies on the part of the international community, Botha felt compelled to resign the presidency in 1989, leaving the way open for de Klerk to take over. De Klerk was able to take advantage of the vacuum left by Botha's resignation and was elected to lead the NP the state presidency, setting the stage for change. Although plans for reform had, arguably, started earlier, during Botha's presidency, it was de Klerk who took action. In a cascade of reforms driven by long-standing international opprobrium for apartheid, mass opposition, and a downward spiraling economy, de Klerk moved to draft a new constitution, remove key elements of racist social segregation in the structures of apartheid, and to open channels of communication with members of the Black opposition movement and the international community. The most critical phase of the transition began when de Klerk reopened, in 1989, discussions with banned opposition organizations and especially his decision to free Nelson Mandela and other key political prisoners. Mandela had previously refused release from prison under the condition to publicly renounce the armed struggle set by Botha. In conversations with de Klerk in which unconditional release was offered, Mandela actually initially demurred, arguing that it was too soon and that the country was not ready. De Klerk nevertheless unbanned the ANC and then released Mandela on February 11, 1990. As the transition to full democracy then began, de Klerk played an increasingly ambiguous role. While on the one hand he ushered in a new postapartheid landscape, on the other hand, he sought to retain protections for Whites that cut against Mandela and the ANC's plan for a single unitary democracy. Mandela became increasingly frustrated with de Klerk's obstructionist efforts aimed at trying to fragment the country during the protracted negotiations during the Convention for a Democratic South Africa (which spanned over two major sessions from 1991 through 1992 and then reformed under the auspices of the Multi Party Negotiating Forum in 1994, which led to democratic elections in 1994), although others such as **Mangosuthu Buthelezi** of the Zulu nationalist Inkatha Freedom Party (IFP) also played a similar role. Indeed, Mandela was incensed by de Klerk's apparent complicity in allowing the so-called third force to destabilize the process through widespread violence in major urban and township areas of the country. Mandela never appeared to accept de Klerk's denials of his role in the violence, nor was he comfortable in sharing the Nobel Peace Prize with him. Mandela, nevertheless, accepted the need for de Klerk to lead

The Defiance Campaign of 1952. *Courtesy of Jurgen Schadeberg.*

otherwise reluctant Whites away from further violence and to accept the transition to full democracy. Accordingly, in a remarkably conciliatory gesture, Mandela, who had won the presidency in 1994, agreed to de Klerk serving as one of two deputy presidents along with **Thabo Mbeki.** Frustrated and cut out of future power, de Klerk withdrew himself and the NP from the coalition government in 1996 and he retired from politics in 1997. He was found guilty by the Truth and Reconciliation Commission (TRC) of gross violations of human rights while president, but this charge was softened on appeal and appeared in the final report of the commission simply as a failure to disclose abuses. Despite their differences, de Klerk spoke highly of Mandela and his work publicly, and attended his funeral in 2013.

F

FISCHER, ABRAM "BRAM" (April 23, 1908–May 8, 1975). Bram Fischer, who ultimately eschewed his family's staunch Afrikaner and National Party (NP)–supporting pedigree, served as a key member of Nelson Mandela's legal team during the infamous **Rivonia Trial** that saw Mandela sentenced to life in prison. During a visit to the Soviet Union in the 1930s while he was studying overseas, Fischer became enamored with communism and joined the South African Communist Party (SACP). Following the death of his wife and fellow communist Molly in a car accident, Bram devoted himself to the SACP and to assisting the **African National Congress** (ANC), all while building a reputation as an excellent corporate lawyer. Indeed, Fischer assisted with drafting various ANC documents, including party policies and the constitution. He later joined the **Congress of Democrats** (COD) and served as

Nelson Mandela returns to his cell on Robben Island, 2012. *Courtesy of Jurgen Schadeberg.*

Mandela and **Walter Sisulu**'s lawyer during the **Defiance Campaign** of 1952. More famously, he was instrumental as a member of the Rivonia Trial defense team, and helped Mandela and others avoid the death penalty. Following the trial, Fischer was charged with violating the Suppression of Communism Act, but eluded capture for a time before being caught in 1966, found guilty, and sentenced to life in prison. After repeated humanitarian appeals because he was suffering from cancer, he was released in 1974 and died a few months later. Nelson Mandela praised his courage and service to the cause of justice and the antiapartheid struggle.

46664. Nelson Mandela's assigned number as a prisoner on Robben Island was based on his arrival date and induction as the 466th prisoner incarcerated there in 1964, thus 46664. As Mandela fought for the dignity and rights of prisoners there, he objected to the dehumanization of people by the application of numbers instead of names. After his release from prison and the end of his presidency, Mandela used the number as a brand for his AIDS charity campaign aimed at educating young people about HIV/AIDS. The 46664 campaign centered on as series charity rock concerts from 2003 to 2008, the first of which was at Green Point Stadium in Cape Town on November 29, 2003 and featured world-renowned musicians and groups such as Queen, U2, Bob Geldof, and South African artists Ladysmith Black Mambazo and Johnny Clegg. The campaign and Mandela's prison number are now part of the intellectual property and branding controlled by the Nelson Mandela Foundation, though the concert series has been ended.

FREEDOM CHARTER. See CONGRESS OF THE PEOPLE AND THE FREEDOM CHARTER

G

GOLDBERG, DENIS (April 11, 1933–). Denis Goldberg, a staunch member of the South African Communist Party (SACP) and leader of the **Congress of Democrats** (COD), was a codefendant at the infamous **Rivonia Trial** where Nelson Mandela was sentenced to life in prison. Raised by communist parents who were Lithuanian Jews who had immigrated to South Africa via the United Kingdom, Goldberg became involved in antiapartheid politics from an early age and had worked for the **Congress of the People** to create alliances among the various opposition organizations. Educated in engineering, he went on to join **Umkhonto We Sizwe (MK)**, the armed wing of the **African National Congress** (ANC), as a technical officer advising about sabotage. Goldberg was instrumental in drafting the plans for Operation Mayibuye, the aspirational plan for countrywide resistance and sabotage that security police found at MK's secret hideout, Liliesleaf Farm. Arrested in the police raid on the farm in 1963, Goldberg offered to take the fall for the plan since he had written most of it, but the others who were arrested, including Mandela, refused. Goldberg was convicted along with Mandela and eight others, but as a White, Goldberg was separated from his Black colleagues and served his twenty-two-year sentence in Pretoria Central Prison while his wife, Esme, fled to exile in the United Kingdom. Finally released in 1985, he left for the United Kingdom, but returned to South Africa in 2002 to serve as advisor to various ANC members of parliament. In 2019, the ANC presented Goldberg with its highest honor, the

Isitwalandwe Medal, for his service to the party and the country.

GORDIMER, NADINE (November 20, 1923–July 13, 2014). A political activist, member of the **African National Congress** (ANC), and internationally acclaimed writer and Nobel Laureate in literature for 2014 (she was one of three—and the only woman—members of the ANC to be Nobel Prize winners alongside Nelson Mandela and **Chief Albert Luthuli**), Nadine Gordimer had an important influence on Mandela from the time they met at the **Rivonia Trial** in 1964. She is perhaps best known for her novels *The Conservationist* (1974), which was a cowinner of the Booker Prize in 1974, and *Burgher's Daughter* (1979), which was, in part, inspired by and modeled on the life of **Bram Fischer**. *Burgher's Daughter* was banned by the government as were other of her works. Mandela, nevertheless, managed to have a copy smuggled to him and read it while imprisoned on Robben Island. He noted that it provided him with insights into the sensitivities of liberal White South Africans. The daughter of a Jewish refugee father from Latvia and an English activist mother, Gordimer engaged in opposition to segregation and apartheid from an early age. Following the detention of a friend and the escalation of censorship and banning of her and other opposition writers' work, Gordimer intensified her antiapartheid stance through both her novels and public speaking. Moreover she fought against censorship as a cofounder of the Congress of South African Writers.

Following the Sharpeville Massacre in 1960, she began following the struggle more closely, including the events surrounding the infamous Rivonia Trial. Gordimer became friends with two of Mandela's lawyers during this period, Bram Fischer and **George Bizos**, and she attended the hearings of the trial. She was, more importantly, along with Mandela friend and biographer Anthony Sampson, involved in editing Mandela's now famous "I am prepared to die" speech (see appendix B) in preparation for his presentation of it from the dock. She spoke out against apartheid and the government in South Africa and around the world, and gave evidence in support of the United Democratic Front (UDF) when members were charged with treason by the state at the infamous Delmas Treason Trial in the mid-1980s. Gordimer remained a long-time supporter of the ANC, but did not become a full member until 1990 as the end of apartheid was in sight, though the organization was still officially banned at the time. Upon his release from prison after twenty-seven years, Gordimer was among the first notable people that Nelson Mandela sought out. Gordimer noted that in a meeting over dinner, Mandela was less interested in discussing her novels than in confiding in her that his marriage to **Winnie Madikizela-Mandela** was over due to her infidelity. The two remained close friends although Gordimer remained aloof from involvement in the ANC government. Indeed, she often critiqued ANC policy and corruption once the party assumed power. Mandela nevertheless praised her cultural contributions to the nation during parliamentary budget debates in 1996. Gordimer also gave a moving keynote speech when Amnesty International conferred the title of Ambassador of Conscience on Mandela in November 2006.

GOVERNMENT OF NATIONAL UNITY. Following Nelson Mandela's release from prison and the protracted negotiations of the Convention for a Democratic South Africa (CODESA), the **African National Congress** (ANC), which won a majority of parliamentary seats in the first all-democratic elections of 1994, agreed to share power in a Government of National Unity (GNU), which lasted from April 27 of 1991 to February 3 of 1997, and through an interim constitution agreed on at CODESA. Article 88 of the GNU interim constitution provided for each party that won twenty or more seats to be granted cabinet appointments. Mandela served as the president, and **Fredrick Willem de Klerk** of the all-White National Party (NP) and **Thabo Mbeki** of the ANC served as deputy presidents. Significantly, **Mangosuthu Buthelezi** of the Inkatha Freedom Party (IFP), which, with the support of "third force" clandestine elements of the NP state-security apparatus had waged a low-intensity war against the ANC and its supporters in the run-up to the elections, was given the cabinet-level post of minister of home affairs. President Mandela shared out the remaining cabinet appointments in an effort to ease the transition to a full, multiparty democracy. A key focus of the GNU was the drafting of a new, permanent constitution which came to fruition as Act No. 108 of 1996, The Constitution of the Republic of South Africa, 1996. De Klerk and the NP then withdrew from the GNU, yet Mandela was able to hold other minority parties within the transitional government until the end of the first parliament in 1999.

H

HEALDTOWN SCHOOL. Named for a then-prominent British Wesleyan politician, James Heald, this comprehensive boarding high school was established at Fort Beaufort in the Transkei in 1855 as part of the colonial vanguard of expansion into the Eastern Cape region by White settlers and Methodist missionaries. Following the educational path of **Justice Dalindyebo** who was four years ahead of him, Nelson Mandela began at Healdtown in 1937 and matriculated with his high-school diploma in 1938. While at Healdtown, Mandela learned both British and **Xhosa** history from his teacher, Mr. Weaver Newana, and he first heard about the then all-but-moribund **African National Congress** (ANC). It was also at Healdtown where Mandela took up boxing, which he would pursue as a sport through much of his young life, and long-distance running, as well as serve as a prefect. During Mandela's time there, Healdtown boasted close to one thousand students and was later the educational home to a number of other important anti-apartheid leaders including Raymond Mahlaba and Robert Sobukwe.

HIV/AIDS. As Nelson Mandela was released from prison, South Africa was confronted by the rapidly spreading epidemic of Human Immunodeficiency Virus (HIV) and the related Acquired Immunodeficiency Syndrome (AIDS). By the end of the 1990s, HIV infection rates started to soar to over 25 percent of the population, among the highest in the world, in a context of poverty, labor migration, and inequality. Without access to affordable pharmaceuticals, millions succumbed to the devastating pandemic, leaving a generation of AIDS orphans. While president, Mandela acknowledged the scope of the problem, and provided some limited funding to address it, his efforts were hampered by politics and the social stigmatization of AIDS patients, and he was criticized for an ineffective response. Among the problems he faced was a sense that the other crises of education, unemployment, inequality, poverty, and lack of health care, all legacies of the apartheid era, were more pressing than the pandemic. Additionally, most South Africans did not want to discuss the disease, seeing it as shameful and a taboo subject. The AIDS crisis worsened as Mandela stepped out of the presidency, allowing **Thabo Mbeki** to succeed in the next election in 1999. Although Mbeki recognized there was a health crisis, he refused to take action and accepted a view of the epidemic as not being caused by the HIV virus that has since been discredited by the scientific community and was labeled as a "denialist." It was only after the Treatment Action Campaign (TAC), established by AIDS activist Zackie Achmat in 1998, lobbied the **African National Congress** (ANC) government that it agreed to provide critically needed treatments to address the epidemic. Once out of the office of the presidency, Mandela more openly supported the AIDS campaign. Donning an HIV-positive T-shirt, Mandela spoke passionately about the need to address the crisis. In 2000, he spoke at an international AIDS conference in Durban and in 2003, the Nelson Mandela Award for Health and Human Rights was given to the TAC. Also in 2003, Mandela lent the prestige of his image to an AIDS charity campaign named "**46664**" for his assigned prisoner number on Robben Island. Mandela furthered his public commitment to dealing with the crisis by announcing that his son, **Makgatho Mandela**, who passed in 2005, had died of complications related to AIDS and he remained dedicated to the cause for the rest of his life.

J

JOFFE, JOEL GOODMAN (BARON JOFFE) (May 12, 1932–June 18, 2017). A human rights lawyer, Joel Joffe was part of the legal team and the lead attorney that defended Nelson Mandela and others accused of sabotage in the **Rivonia Trial**. Born in South Africa to a Jewish Lithuanian father and a Palestinian mother, Joffe earned his law degree from the University of the Witwatersrand in 1955. He moved to the United Kingdom in 1965, not long after Mandela was imprisoned for life and there rose to prominence in the financial services industry and for his philanthropy. In 2000, he was made a life peer of the United Kingdom as Baron Joffe. Along with fellow attorneys **George Bizos** and **Bram Fischer**, Joffe played a key role in developing the legal strategy that allowed Mandela and his codefendants at the Rivonia Trial to escape the death penalty, which many feared would be the outcome of the trial. He and fellow attorney Bizos were featured in the documentary "Life Is Wonderful" (directed by Nick Stadlen, 2017).

JOHANNESBURG. The largest city in South Africa during Nelson Mandela's life, Johannesburg had its origins during the 1880s in the highly exploitive mining industry that relied so heavily on African migrant workers from the rural areas of southern and central Africa. Also known as "Egoli," a vernacular reference to the importance of gold mining, Johannesburg was already a deeply segregated city by the time of Mandela's arrival in the **Alexandra Township**. Subjected to various pernicious legal and economic constraints there, Africans struggled to gain footholds in property rights and employment but also managed to create vibrant havens where music and African culture thrived, such as Sophiatown. Prior to his incarceration, from 1942–1960, Mandela made his home in the famous Johannesburg township of **Soweto** on Vilakazi Street. He returned to stay briefly in this house, now the Nelson Mandela National Museum, after his release from prison in 1990.

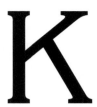

K

KATHRADA, AHMED MOHAMED "KATHY" (August 21, 1929–March 28, 2017). The son of Gujurati, South Asian immigrant parents who settled in the small northwest province town of Schweizer-Reneke, Ahmed Kathrada was a leading Indian South African member of the **African National Congress** (ANC) and South African Communist Party (SACP). Kathy, as he was affectionately called by Nelson Mandela and other friends of these organizations, had an early start in opposition politics when he joined the SACP Youth League at the age of twelve. Thereafter, he was deeply influenced by South African and Transvaal Indian Congress leaders **Yusuf Dadoo**, **Ismail Meer**, and **Yusuf Cachalia**. Their early work on the passive-resistance campaign against passes for Indians and the "Ghetto Act," by which the state sought to curtail participation in government through control of Asian access to land, inspired Kathrada to join the ranks of those mobilizing to protest. He joined thousands of others in mass action, and was arrested and jailed for this, as well as other acts of civil disobedience and protest. It was during these protests in the late 1940s and into the 1950s that collaborations between the ANC and the SAIC emerged. Although Mandela, **Oliver Tambo**, and other members of the ANC Youth League initially opposed collaboration, to the extent that Mandela actually shoved Cachalia off a platform when he attempted to speak at a joint meeting, **Walter Sisulu** and others convinced Mandela that cooperation was the only way forward. By this time, Mandela was studying and practic-

ing law and he began fraternizing with SAIC leaders, such as Ismail Meer, who were fellow law students at the University of the Witwatersrand, and Kathrada was among the youth who joined their meetings and political discussions. Following travel and attendance at various Left youth movements in Eastern Europe, Kathrada returned to South Africa where he helped forge the alliance between the SAIC and the ANC that led to the joint **Defiance Campaign** of the 1950s, where mass action and passive resistance challenged the state to repeal apartheid laws. He was arrested and banned repeatedly by the government over the next few years. Owing to his work with Mandela and others with helping organize the **Congress of the People**, he was charged and tried alongside 155 other defendants in the **Treason Trial** of 1956. As with Mandela and other coaccused, the charges against Kathrada were eventually dropped, but he had, by then, come to the notice of state security. Further police harassment, arrests, and banning orders made life for Kathrada intolerable and undermined his work with the resistance movement. By 1963, he defied his house arrest and went underground to operate clandestinely with other ANC operatives who were working out of the supposedly secret location at Liliesleaf Farm in Rivonia. It was there that state security police raided the farm and arrested Kathrada along with other members of the **Umkhonto We Sizwe (MK)** high command, including **Lionel "Rusty" Bernstein**, Bob Hepple, **Govan Mbeki**, Raymond Mhlaba, and Sisulu. Mandela, who was already in jail at the time of the raid, would be tried alongside Kathrada and the others owing to incriminating documents found at Liliesleaf Farm. At the ensuing infamous **Rivonia Trial**, Kathrada eschewed offers to be separated as an Indian South African from the other accused in hopes of a lighter sentence. He maintained his commitment to solidarity among all races in the resistance. Kathrada was sentenced to life imprisonment and was sent to Robben Island as prisoner 468/64, where he spent the next eighteen years with Mandela and numerous other political prisoners. While there, Kathrada contributed to the lively political debates among members of the ANC and SACP as well as helped safeguard one of Mandela's autobiography manuscripts. As with Mandela, he also studied and earned a number of bachelor's degrees through the University of South Africa, the correspondence institution at which

so many political prisoners earned degrees. After being moved to Pollsmoor Prison on the mainland and serving another eight years in jail, he was released on October 15, 1989, to a country-wide, popular welcome. The ANC conferred on him the Isitwalandwe Award, its highest honor. Kathrada then served as head of public relations for the ANC as it transitioned into power and he was elected to the party's National Executive Committee multiple times. Mandela then appointed him as political advisor and to the newly created post of Parliamentary Counsellor in the Office of the President. Kathrada also attend Mandela and Graça Machel's small, intimate wedding ceremony in 1998. He left service in the government in 1999 but continued to work to promote a greater understanding of the history of Robben Island and the struggle, as well as to write about and collaborate with Mandela.

L

LUTHULI, NKOSI (CHIEF) ALBERT JOHN MVUMBI (1898–July 21, 1967). Chief Luthuli served as President-General of the **African National Congress** (ANC) from December 1952 until his death in 1967. He was a gifted leader who straddled the time and styles of both the early conservative membership of the party and the later more radical youth such as Nelson Mandela. Luthuli, who hailed from the isiZulu-speaking ethnic group, was born in what is now Zimbabwe, but following the death of his father when he was ten, the family moved to their ancestral home near Groutville in KwaZulu-Natal. From then, he was raised in various Christian mission stations and schools, including the celebrated Ohlange Institute established by the Reverend Dr. John Dube, who was the founding president of the South African National Native Congress, a position that Luthuli would later fill under the guise of the organization's new name, the ANC. Luthuli declined the opportunity to attend the **University of Fort Hare**, opting rather to undertake a comparatively well-paid job as a teacher in order to support his family. He was then elected to serve as chief of the *Amkholwa* (Christian African) community in Groutville, near Stanger, Natal. This was both an honorific and civic leadership role. The unavoidable effects of segregation and racial oppression in the country, however, prompted him to engage in opposition politics, and he joined the ANC in 1944. Thereafter, he played a leading role in collaborations with other opposition organizations such as the South African Indian Congress (SAIC) for mass resistance. The state deposed him as chief for these activities and he would later suffer various banning orders. In 1952, he was elected to lead the ANC and so came to hold authority over the party as Nelson Mandela was just coming of age in the ANC Youth League. Luthuli joined in many mass-action campaigns including the **Defiance Campaign** and, in 1956, became, along with Mandela, one of the 156 **Treason Trial** defendants. As Luthuli grappled with the growing divide between Africanist and nonracialist and communist influences in the opposition movement, the ANC youth were moving toward a more radical agenda. By 1960, Mandela and others had determined that in the face of violent government repression, they would embark on the armed struggle. It is not clear if Mandela received approval from President Luthuli for the formation of **Umkhonto We Sizwe (MK)**, but the move to armed struggle clearly did not sit comfortably with Luthuli and he distanced himself from the party afterward. Nevertheless, he played a key role in shaping the ANC's policy and practice of peaceful, passive mass resistance prior to its embrace of the armed struggle. It was for this stance in his opposition to apartheid that he was awarded the Nobel Peace Prize in 1960, an honor that Mandela would share some thirty years later but by having followed a different path.

M

MACHEL, GRAÇA SIMBINE (October 17, 1945–). Nelson Mandela married Graça Simbine Machel, then age fifty-two, on his eightieth birthday on July 18, 1998. She was his third wife, following his divorces from **Evelyn Mase** in 1958 and **Winnie Mandela** in 1996, and is the only woman so far to have served as the first lady of two nations, South Africa and Mozambique. Machel shared many things with Mandela, including being raised in the Methodist faith, the spirit of resistance, and the experiences of a fellow freedom fighter against White and colonial oppression. Born in Gaza Province, Mozambique (then a colony of Portugal) in 1945, Graça Machel engaged in the liberation struggle for her country from an early age. One of six children of a peasant family and father who received a mission education and became a Methodist minister, but who died just a few weeks before she was born, Graça won a Methodist scholarship to study languages at Lisbon University in Portugal. While there, she pursued leftist anticolonial politics and joined *Frente de Libertação de Moçambique* (FRELIMO, the Mozambique Liberation Front), which sought the national liberation of her country from Portuguese colonial rule. In 1973, she returned to Africa, first to Tanzania and then Mozambique, underwent military training, and took up the armed struggle as she took on leadership of the FRELIMO headquarters in exile. She then met and married Samora Machel, commander of FRELIMO and later president of an independent Mozambique. Graça became minister of education for the FRELIMO government and was by all accounts very successful in the development of education in Mozambique as well as champion of welfare for child victims of war, a cause she continues to serve through the Nelson Mandela Foundation. Mandela first met Graça in 1990 when he visited the frontline states (those neighboring African states that had helped press for the end of apartheid) after his release from prison. They had corresponded in the past after Samora Machel was killed in a 1986 plane crash in which the South African state was suspected of involvement. Following his trip to Mozambique, his estrangement from his wife Winnie had grown more difficult, publicly and politically, and Mandela appeared to find friendship, succor, and mutual attraction with Graça. Indeed, their private relationship quickly developed into a public romance. Graça was credited with creating a more open, loving, and happy home life for Mandela compared to previous marriages, which had occurred during times of great political tension and oppression in the era of segregation and apartheid. Despite the enormous demands on their time from their respective nations (as Samora's widow, Graça still held great popular appeal in Mozambique) and apparent resentment from both his former wives, Mandela and Graça shared a happy marriage until his death. She was, with Mandela, a cofounder of the Elders group and continues to be active in development work in Africa through the Africa Progress Panel.

MADIKIZELA-MANDELA, NOMZAMO WINIFRED ZANYIWE (September 26, 1936–April 2, 2018). Better known as "Winnie" and often referred to by her supporters as the "Mother of the Nation" and as the "Queen of Africa" by many African Americans for her work in the liberation struggle, she was Nelson Mandela's second wife from 1958 to 1996. A leading anti-apartheid activist with rural roots in the Transkei region similar to Nelson, she faced considerable pressure and harassment from the state and was imprisoned for her political activities. Initially celebrated for her public challenges to state policies and her advocacy on behalf of her husband, she became among the most controversial figures in South African politics and eventually an embarrassment to Nelson, leading to their divorce. Born in Bizana, part of the Pondoland area of the Transkei, her **Xhosa** name, Nomzamo, refers to striving through struggles. Raised by Methodist-mission-educated parents, Columbus and Gertrude Madikizela, schoolteachers who were strict disciplinarians, Winnie was known to have rebelled from an early age, a trait she carried with her into adulthood. After her mother passed away when she was nine years old, Winnie took on more family responsibilities and focused on her studies at Methodist mission schools. Her academic success there led to her admission in 1953 to the Jan Hofmeyr School of Social Work where she did research on African infant mortality in **Alexandra** and from which she was among the first African women in South Africa to graduate. She embarked on a successful career as a social worker at Baragwanath Hospital, Soweto's largest medical facility for Africans, and her notoriety attracted the attention of the African press as well as **Kaiser Matanzima**, Nelson Mandela's elder nephew. Having acquired an urban sophistication, Winnie demurred at Matanzima's efforts to win her hand as his second wife, a common practice among rural African chiefs and elders, when Nelson began to take an interest in her. Nelson met Winnie during the stressful and chaotic days of the **Treason Trial** while he was juggling court appearances during the day and managing his legal practice with his partner and fellow accused, **Oliver Tambo**, in the evenings and on weekends. Nelson's first marriage to **Evelyn Mase** was practically over when Tambo and his then-fiancée **Adelaide Tambo** (née Tshukudu),

a nurse at Baragwanath and friend of Winnie's, introduced Winnie to him. Their courtship was fraught with complications and clandestine meetings because Nelson was under a banning order that prevented him from associating with other political activists and Winnie was already involved with opposition politics and activism. Nevertheless, Nelson's passion prevailed and, following his formal divorce from Evelyn on March 19, 1958, they married on June 14, 1958, in Bizana. They wed during the height of the Treason Trial and because of his political celebrity, the wedding caught the national interest and was reported in *Drum* magazine. During the tumultuous early years of their marriage, Winnie and Nelson had two daughters, **Zenani Mandela-Dlamini**, born in 1959, and **Zindziswa Mandela-Hlongwane**, born in 1960. Zenani was born just a few months after Winnie was released from jail after her arrest for involvement with ANC Women's League protest against the pass laws. Not long after that, in 1961, the ANC executive directed her husband to go underground during his Black Pimpernel phase, and then leave the country on a training mission. After Nelson's return, arrest, and long-term imprisonment in 1962, Winnie faced raising both daughters on her own while she contended with her own career of political activism and concomitant government harassment. In December of 1962, not long before Nelson was transferred to the Robben Island Prison, the government feared Winnie would take up a leadership role in the ANC, and placed her under a banning order restricting her to **Johannesburg**, making it all the more difficult for her to visit her husband. Thereafter, the security police beset Winnie and her family with ever-more intense harassment and banning orders. The children were hounded from every school they tried to attend, leading Winnie to seek the assistance of Helen Joseph to help arrange for their education in neighboring Swaziland. She retold many of the travails of being separated from Nelson in her book, *Part of My Soul Went with Him*. In May of 1969, the government invoked the sweeping Terrorism Act, No 83 of 1967 to arrest Winnie and incarcerate her for over a year, her longest sentence, an experience that included two hundred days of solitary confinement and torture, which she chronicled in her book *491 Days: Prisoner Number 1323/69*. Upon her release, she endured further state security surveillance and persecutions, arrests, imprisonments, and banning orders. These culminated in 1977 with her banishment to a tiny house without electricity or running water in the rural Black township of Phathakahle adjacent to the Whites-only town of Brandtford, over 250 miles from her Johannesburg home. Under her banning order and exile, she could not leave the district except for the rare occasions when she was permitted to visit her husband in prison, although it was a long and costly odyssey for her to make the trip to Robben Island. Winnie, who was accompanied during part of the banishment by her daughter Zindzi, nevertheless, maintained her strong antiapartheid stance and challenges to the state. When, in 1986, her banishment was lifted and she returned to the home she and Nelson had shared, however briefly, on Vilakazi Street in Orlando West, **Soweto**, she arrived as a leading icon of the liberation struggle with massive popular support among Africans radicalized by the continued oppression and state violence of apartheid, especially during the Soweto uprising in 1976 where thousands of school students led protests against the insufficiencies of apartheid education. It was during the ensuing dramatic escalation of mass resistance and the response of brutal state repression that Winnie and some other members of the opposition began to engage in extreme political tactics and violence. By the mid-1980s, mass opposition to the state had spread and taken on an aggressive approach that the United Democratic Front (UDF) and its successor the Mass Democratic Movement struggled to contain. Among the strategies was a new approach aimed at making the townships "ungovernable," which included various young "comrades" establishing kangaroo courts to take justice into their own hands. Winnie was often at the forefront of actions that sometimes pitted groups against each other in a spiral that the international press and critics of the ANC often referred to as "Black on Black" violence. In a fateful public statement that spread around the world, Win-

nie endorsed the use of "necklacing," a ghastly practice whereby people accused of being traitors to the liberation struggle were killed by hanging a gasoline-soaked car tire around their neck and setting it alight. Thereafter, Winnie grew more violent and seemingly irrational as she surrounded herself with the infamous **Mandela United Football Club** (MUFC), a group of erstwhile soccer players who took on a thuggish role as her personal bodyguard and enforcers. Directed by Winnie and led by Jerry Richardson, MFUC became notorious for terrorizing and torturing young township residents accused of crimes or of being police informants for the state. Nelson, still in prison but able to communicate through various channels with ANC leaders, learned of Winnie's aberrant behavior and convened a crisis committee in a vain effort to restrain his wife. In a personal meeting with Winnie, he admonished her to disband the MUFC as well as to disavow an agreement she had tried to make with a Black American entrepreneur, Robert Brown, to profit off a copyright to market Mandela's name. Things came to a head in 1989 when it came to light that Winnie was complicit in the murder, among perhaps a dozen others, by the MUCF of "Stompie" Moeketse Seipei, a township youth accused of being a police informant. She had also apparently ordered the killing of Dr. Abu-Bakr Asvat, a supporter of the antiapartheid movement who often served as physician to ANC and MK comrades in need. At Winnie's request, Dr. Asvat had attended to Stompie after he had been tortured by the MUFC and so he had firsthand knowledge of the crimes and that the boy had been in Winnie's custody. The crisis committee condemned and censured Winnie, though Nelson still found it difficult to separate his love and loyalty for her from the need to distance himself from the clear evidence of her appalling criminal behavior. While the mainstream antiapartheid movement and the ANC executive in exile rebuked Winnie, because of her status and marriage to Nelson she ultimately escaped prosecution for the murder of Stompie. She was, however, convicted for kidnapping though Chief Justice Michael Corbett, in a move many thought to be in political deference to her husband Nelson, granted her suspended sentence and 15,000 Rand (approximately $30,000 at the time) fine. Other members of the MFUC were convicted of multiple counts of murder. Ten years later, the Truth and Reconciliation Commission (TRC), found Winnie responsible for gross violations of human rights in the case of Stompie Seipei as well as the disappearance of others. In a final urging by the TRC chair, Archbishop Desmond Tutu, Winnie offered a brief and unemotional apology to Stompie's mother and, under the protocols of the TRC, the matter was closed. Nelson's continued support of her, and his refusal to accept her wrongdoings, including her well-known affair with her lawyer, Dali Mpofu, persisted. Winnie accompanied Nelson, arm-in-arm, on his release from Victor Verster Prison in 1990 and thereafter, he ensured that senior ANC leaders appeared in support at her kidnapping and murder trial. Moreover Nelson helped her secure key leadership roles in the ANC as head of social welfare and ultimately, her election as president of the ANC Women's League. In 1992, however, when Winnie's role in directing the murder of Dr. Asvat came to light, and with her evermore flagrant public displays of her affair with Mpofu, Nelson finally broke. In a rare press statement about his private life, he announced both his continued love and devotion for Winnie and his reluctant decision to separate from her. They were finally formally divorced in 1996. Winnie remained popular with many of the rank-and-file of the ANC and, in 1994, she was elected to parliament and appointed as minister of arts, culture, science, and technology in the first democratically elected ANC government. She remained a deeply controversial figure in South African politics thereafter as she was mired in repeated corruption scandals and censured by many in the ANC. In 2003, she was convicted of multiple counts of fraud and theft, some of which were overturned on appeal. After receiving a suspended sentence, she was forced to resign her parliamentary seat and all her leadership positions in the ANC. She rebounded, however, and was reelected to parliament and to the ANC executive, serving until her death. Winnie continued with her political activism including advocat-

ing for immigrant rights and treatment for AIDS. Following Nelson's death in 2013, however, she and her daughters, Zenani and Zindzi, became embroiled in a bitter fight to gain control of the Mandela ancestral home in the Transkei, pitting them against other members of the family from Nelson's first marriage. The case was eventually dismissed in 2016, and Winnie fell ill and died in April 2018. As with her life, the funeral was a very political affair in which tensions within the ANC resurfaced.

MAHARAJ, SATHYANDRANATH RAGU-NANAN "MAC" (April 22, 1935–). A member of the National Executive Committee of the **African National Congress** (ANC), South African Communist Party (SACP), and a leader in its military wing, **Umkhonto We Sizwe (MK)**. The son of a South Asian South African family from Newcastle, Natal, he was educated in Durban but apartheid limits on education for Blacks there led him to pursue a law degree in the United Kingdom from 1957–1962. Maharaj was an important strategist and key underground agent for the ANC. During the 1960s, after the ANC's declaration of an armed struggle, he engaged in planning and carrying out acts of sabotage against the apartheid state. Caught and prosecuted by the state for sabotage at the "Little Rivonia Trial" along with five other members of MK, he was sentenced and served twelve years in the Robben Island Prison alongside Nelson Mandela from July of 1964 until December of 1976. It was during that time in incarceration that he built a friendship with Mandela—he referred to Maharaj as "neef" (Afrikaans for "nephew")—as they and other political prisoners were compelled to do hard labor in the island's lime quarry. Maharaj took part in many clandestine policy discussions among the imprisoned ANC leaders. He was, importantly, instrumental in transcribing and then smuggling out of the prison much of what would become Mandela's autobiography, *Long Walk to Freedom*. Indeed, the Maharaj manuscript became even more critical after prison guards discovered in the prison garden and confiscated Mandela's own long-hand original. Moreover Maharaj collected further essays about the struggle written by political prisoners while on Robben Island, Mandela included, and published these as *Reflections in Prison: Voices from the South African Liberation Struggle.* Following his release from prison, the government maintained a ban on Maharaj for five years, limiting his movements and undermining his ability to work. In July of 1977, the ANC then sent Maharaj to Lusaka, Zambia, where he worked for the organization in exile. Among his achievements there was his elevation to the National Executive Committee of the ANC and helping carry out Operation Vula, which established communications with Mandela in jail, and was intended to secrete exiled operatives into South Africa across the border from various frontline states to serve as leaders in armed insurrection if efforts for a negotiated settlement failed. In 1986, as part of Operation Vula, he returned to South Africa and worked underground to prepare for the return of exiled

ANC leaders. After his release from prison, Mandela directed Maharaj to continue with the operation. In 1990, however, Maharaj and some forty other ANC operatives were arrested and he was charged, among other things, with terrorism for his role in Operation Vula. The state dropped all charges against Maharaj and the others as part of agreements leading to the final negotiated settlement for a democratic South Africa. By that time, Maharaj had openly declared himself to be a member of the SACP. He remained a close confidant of Mandela's and Mandela appointed him minister of transport in the first democratically elected ANC government in 1994.

MANDELA'S AFRICA TOUR 1962. On January 11, 1962, Nelson Mandela, who had been operating undercover under the pseudonym **David Motsamayi**, left South Africa

Courtyard at Robben Island Prison where Nelson Mandela hid the manuscript to his autobiography, *Long Walk to Freedom. Courtesy of Aran MacKinnon.*

for Botswana (then British Bechuanaland) to embark on a training and fundraising overseas tour. The **African National Congress (ANC)** executive had ordered this trip in part as a response to an invitation from the newly formed Pan African Freedom Movement for East, Central, and Southern Africa to their conference in Addis Ababa, Ethiopia. By that time, the ANC had been banned and Mandela was a fugitive from state security police, known in the press as the elusive "Black Pimpernel." Following a secret consultation with then-ANC president **Chief Albert Luthuli**, who had recently received the Nobel Peace Prize for his work in opposing apartheid, Mandela received forged documents and funds in preparation for the trip. In addition to his trying to represent the ANC at the conference, Mandela was also to seek out financial and diplomatic support from as many willing African states as he could; to receive training in military tactics and sabotage techniques; to establish ANC training bases in countries willing to host them; and then to meet with key ANC leaders in exile including **Oliver Tambo**, who was by then set up in London. The guiding principle for the mission was the newly adopted decision to take up and armed struggle and the need for the new armed wing of the party, **Umkhonto We Sizwe (MK)**, to develop capacity under Mandela's leadership. Mandela also wanted to bolster the ANC's image across the continent in a bid to win over more popular support from the growing Pan African Congress (PAC). Mandela was able to take advantage of a "pipeline" of road and air travel for political refugees out of South Africa that was partly aided and abetted by British intelligence operatives in Botswana who wanted access to information about the newly established Republic of South Africa that had broken away from the Commonwealth. Once across the border in Botswana, Mandela and fellow member of the ANC, Joe Matthews, caught a flight to Dar-el-Salaam, Tanzania on January 19 of 1962, where they met and discussed strategy with the great hero of African nationalism, President Julius Nyerere. Nyerere recommended that Mandela seek military training in Ethiopia. Mandela then travelled to Accra in Ghana to await a visa to travel to Addis Ababa, Ethiopia. While in Ethiopia, he was able to meet with Emperor Haile Selassie I, a revered figure of African resistance and gave a speech at an international conference where he outlined the history and policies of the ANC. After touring various military bases in Ethiopia, Mandela received pledges of support and invitations for members of ANC to receive military training, and was given £5,000 to support the ANC. He then flew on the Cairo, Egypt, on February 12, 1962, with Tambo and **Robert Resha**, another MK operative, where they met with representatives from a range of socialist and communist states including Cuba, Czechoslovakia, China, and the German Democratic Republic. While Tambo returned to London, Mandela went on to Tunisia and Morocco, arriving there on March 6, 1962. While in Tunisia, president Bourguiba provided another £5,000 and pledges of other military support and training for the ANC. Later in March, Mandela was hosted by the leader of Algeria's resistance movement in Casablanca, Morocco, Dr. Bouyali Mustafa of the National Liberation Front. He sent Mandela to their training camps in eastern Morocco, near the border with Algeria. It was in Morocco that Mandela first learned to fire a gun, and he began training with various rifles and pistols. In later March, Mandela then traveled through and did fundraising in various West African states including Sierra Leone, Liberia, Ghana, and Nigeria. He also received funds from Liberian president William Tubman and Guinean president Ahmed Sékou Touré before travelling on to Senegal. President Leopold Senghor of Senegal then paid the airfare and provided a diplomatic passport in the name of David Motsamyi for Mandela to travel to London in the United Kingdom where he met again with Tambo and with **Mary Benson** for a brief diplomatic tour. Following that tour, he returned to Ethiopia to continue military training in weapons, tactics, and explosives. While there, Colonel Birou Tadesse oversaw his rigorous training, which included daily marches of fifteen miles or more in full uniform. After eight weeks of training, the ANC executive suddenly called Mandela back to South Africa. They felt they needed his leadership in the escalating armed struggle and were also concerned with rumors floated by the PAC that he had drifted back to a Black nationalist–only stance and so abandoned the ANC's policy of nonracialism and multiparty collaboration. On the eve of his departure, Colonel Tadesse gave Mandela a gift of a pistol, most likely a Makarov, and two hundred rounds of ammunition. Mandela was particularly proud of this weapon and sported it conspicuously along with his military uniform on his return to South Africa. He later remembered burying the pistol somewhere on the grounds of Liliesleaf Farm, not long before he was captured by South African police in Howick, KwaZulu-Natal.

MANDELA-AMUAH, PUMLA MAKAZIWE (1954–). Named after her elder sister who died at the age of nine months, Pumla Makaziwe "Maki" Mandela is the only surviving child of Nelson Mandela and **Evelyn Mase**. Nelson encouraged her to get a good education and sent her to Waterford Kamhlaba, an international boarding school in neighboring Swaziland. As with her father, she attended the **University of Fort Hare**, and then with a Fulbright Scholarship, she went on to earn a PhD in anthropology from the University of Massachusetts in the United States. From the time of her father's arrest in 1962 until his release in 1990, Maki had to cope with the stress and upheavals that came with being the child of a political prisoner. She made her first visits to see her father on Robben Island at the age of sixteen, and struggled to keep regular contact because of pernicious government regulations. She endured further strains in their relationship because of tensions after her father's divorce from her mother, Evelyn, and his new marriage to **Winnie Mandikezela-Mandela** as well as competing with her new half-sisters **Zenani Dlamini** and **Zindsziwa Mandela**. She was not reconciled with her father until after his divorce from Winnie in 1996. Maki eventually took on a greater leadership role for her section of the family following her father's death and went on to help promote his artwork in galleries and sales around the world. She is also the founder of the House of Mandela wine label and business.

MANDELA-DLAMINI, ZENANI (February 4, 1959–). Born in **Soweto** just a few months after her mother, **Winnie Madikizela-Mandela**, was released from prison having been jailed for having opposed apartheid, and while her father, Nelson, was undergoing prosecution at the **Treason Trial**, Zenani grew up in tumultuous times. She and her younger sister **Zindziswa Mandela-Hlongwane** faced repeated disruptions to their lives and schooling. By the age of four, Zenani's father was sent to prison on a life sentence, and her mother faced incessant harassment from the state security police. When Nelson went underground, she could only meet him clandestinely at Liliesleaf Farm. Zenani and her sister were hounded out of a number of schools, compelling their parents to call upon Helen Joseph, a leading White antiapartheid activist, and his lawyer, **George Bizos**, to assist with arranging for the girls to attend the first nonracial private international school, Waterford Kamhlaba United World College of Southern Africa in neighboring Swaziland. She was not allowed to see her father until the age of sixteen in 1975, when the state finally granted permission for brief visits, and so she was estranged from him until his release in 1990. Two years later, at the age of eighteen, Zenani became a princess of the Swazi royal family when she married Prince Thumbumuzi Dlamini, a son of King Sobhuza of Swaziland and elder brother to the current king, Mswati III. She was then able to leverage her status as princess with diplomatic credentials to gain a special visit with her baby daughter and husband to see her father in the Robben Island Prison in 1977. Following his election as the first democratic president of South Africa and the end of his marriage to Winnie, Nelson chose Zenani to serve as a substitute first lady at his inauguration and at other affairs of state until he married **Graça Machel**. Zenani then was appointed in 2012 as South African ambassador to Argentina. She continues to serve in the diplomatic corps for the country, most recently as high commissioner to Mauritius.

MANDELA-HLONGWANE, ZINDZISWA (December 23, 1960–). The second of two children to **Winnie Madikizela-Mandela** and

Nelson Mandela, Zindziswa, or "Zindzi" as she is popularly known, was younger sister to **Zenani Mandela-Dlamini**. As with her sister, she was born into tumultuous times and trying experiences as both her mother and father faced intense state security harassment and prosecutions for their work in the anti-apartheid movement. The year she was born, the government banned the **African National Congress** (ANC), and her father helped establish the underground armed wing of the party, **Umkhonto We Sizwe (MK)**. In her younger days, Zindzi had to accompany her mother, Winnie, for eight years during her banning and exile to Brantford. Unable to remain at any state-sponsored schools in South Africa because of intimidation by the police and White administrators, she joined her sister at the private international school Waterford Kamhlaba United World College of Southern Africa in Swaziland. She later studied law and earned a Bachelor of Arts degree at the University of Cape Town. Zindzi was unable to see her father from the age of eighteen months until she was fifteen, owing to his imprisonment on Robben Island. As she grew up, Zindzi served as a prominent antiapartheid activist, often in the same mold as her mother, and in 1978 she published a book of poetry, *Black As I Am*, about the struggle, which also included photographs by the celebrated South African photographer Peter Magubane. In 1985, when Nelson rejected then-President **P. W. Botha**'s offer of release from prison on condition that he publicly renounce the use of violence in the liberation struggle, it was Zindzi who spoke his words. According to South Africa law at the time and because he was a banned "terrorist," her father could not speak himself or be quoted in public. Zindzi was later implicated in various criminal activities associated with her mother and the activities of the **Mandela United Football Club** (MUFC). She was at the center of further controversy when American boxing promoter Duane Moody sued her successfully for $7.5 million. The case involved her failure to fulfill a contract to arrange for a boxing match between world-renowned fighters Floyd Mayweather and Manny Pacuiao as part of her father Nelson's birthday celebration

in 2011. Zindzi remained loyal to her mother throughout her life, and often defended Winnie during repeated accusations and prosecutions for criminal behavior, in some of which Zindzi was herself was implicated. She nevertheless remained an ANC party loyalist and in 2014 was appointed as South African ambassador to Denmark.

MANDELA, MAGKATHO LEWANIKA (June 26, 1950–January 6, 2005). The second-born son of Nelson Mandela and his first wife **Evelyn Mase**, Magkatho Mandela died at the age of fifty-five from complications arising from an **HIV/AIDS**-related illness. He was, along with **Madiba Thembekile Mandela** and **Pumla Makaziwe "Maki" Mandela-Amuah**, one the three of Nelson Mandela's and his first wife, Evelyn Mase's children to survive into adulthood. Makaziwe Mandela, a daughter, died in 1948 at the age of nine months. Despite Mandela's divorce in 1958 from Evelyn, their children Magkathao and his sister Maki visited him in prison on Robben Island many times over the years. Tensions for Magkatho within the family increased over the years as the strain of his father's incarceration took a toll, and he felt a great deal of pressure from his father to succeed following his elder brother Thembekile's death in a car accident in 1969. Magkatho eventually embraced his studies and, at his father's urging, he embarked on a career as an attorney. In a departure from his previous relative silence as president on the AIDS crisis in South Africa, Nelson publicly disclosed that Magkatho had died of the disease. This marked the beginning of Nelson's more open, public effort to destigmatize AIDS and to help fund research to find a cure. It was later revealed that Makgatho's second wife, Zondi Mandela, had died of pneumonia likely caused by AIDS-related complications at the age of forty-six on July 13, 2003. Makgatho was survived by four sons, Mandla, from his first marriage, and Ndaba, twenty-one; Mbuso, thirteen; and Andile, eleven, from his marriage to Zondi. Magkatho's family was further mired in controversy when his son, and Nelson's grandson, Mandla Mandela, sought to evict relatives of his grandmother, Evelyn

Mase, from the house she and Nelson had shared when ownership of the house passed to Mandla on his father's death. Mandla did inherit and serves in the role of clan chief that his father declined and which Nelson was otherwise supposed to inherit.

MANDELA, MPHAKANYISWA HENRY GADLA (1880–1930).

Henry Gadla Mandela, Nelson's father, was descended from the **Thembu** royal family through the *ixhiba* (from isiZulu and isiXhosa for smaller or "left hand" house) that provided only for morganatic inheritance of the title and role of royal advisor but not royal titles. Henry, accordingly, served as the principal counselor to the regent **Nkosi** (paramount **chief**) **Jongitaba Dalindyebo**. He also was subsumed, as many African traditional leaders were compelled to, in the structures of the colonial system established by the British. As a chief and an officially recognized "headman" of the Mveso village along the Mbashe river in the Transkei region, Henry served for a time in an ambiguous role as an advocate for his village and people while simultaneously having to carry out government policies and orders. He also had a seat on the Transkeian Territories General Council, a combined White and African advisory body to the South African government. In 1926, in his capacity as chief, Henry apparently enforced a law to limit some leading men of the chiefdom from occupying communal land in excessive ways. The men challenged the order and complained to the British magistrate, accusing Henry of corruption. Despite Henry's defense in a trial, the magistrate overturned customary law in support of the accusers and dismissed Henry from his position, thus stripping the Mandela family of its authority and rights to land. The chiefship was only restored to the Mandela family in 2006 when the postapartheid government appointed Nelson's grandson, Mandlesizwe Mandela, to the position. Nelson himself recalled the episode frequently as an example of family resistance to White oppression and as an inspiration for traditional African law and values. Following the dismissal, Nelson and his sisters left the comparative comfort of the Mveso home to live at his mother's kraal (family home consisting of Thembu huts and cattle enclosure) and family at Qunu. In keeping with amaXhosa and Thembu customs of polygamy, Henry had four wives and it was the third of these, **Nonqaphi Fanny Nosekeni Mandela**, who was Nelson's mother. Nelson noted his father had thirteen children with his four wives; nine girls and four boys, of which he was the youngest boy, but was the eldest child of the "right hand house" through which inheritance of titles passed. Three of the girls were direct siblings of Nelson's by his mother; Baliwe, Constance Mbekeni, and Makhutswana. Henry's children with his other wives, Nelson's half-siblings, were sisters Leabie Piliso, Nothusile Bhulehluth, and Mabel Notancu Ntimakhwe, and brothers Mhlalwa Mandela, Nomabandla Mandela, and Daligqili Mandela. Henry also remained a follower of Thembu spiritual customs and beliefs, although his wife Nonqaphi converted to Christianity while Nelson was young, and Henry agreed to Nelson, from the age of eight, attending the Methodist mission school at Qunu. Following his dismissal as chief, Henry's health deteriorated, and he passed away likely from tuberculosis, a common ailment among Africans in South Africa, in 1930 while Nelson was still a young boy. As arranged by his father before his death, Nelson was then sent to live with chief Jongitaba Dalindyebo at **Mqhekezweni, the "Great Place"** to be educated in Thembu customary leadership.

MANDELA, NONQAPHI FANNY NOSEKENI (date of birth unknown–September 1968).

Nelson Mandela's mother, Nonqaphi Fanny Nosekeni, was the third of four wives of **Mphakanyiswa Henry Gadla Mandela**, the chief of Mveso village in the Transkei. Family friends George and Benjamin Mbekela introduced Nonqaphi to the Methodist brand of Christianity, and she embraced the faith and culture to the extent that she took the Christian name "Fanny," began wearing European-style dress, and convinced Nelson's father, Henry, that their children should be educated at the local mission school near her home at Qunu. Although Nelson remained close to his mother and appreciated her Christian values and stories of **Xhosa** lore, he was also raised, as was the custom among polygamous Thembu families, in part by his other mothers, his father's three other wives. After Henry was deposed as chief, Nelson and his sisters were sent to live at Fanny's family kraal at Qunu where he experienced a more modest rural life than at his father's somewhat grander home. By the age of twelve, following his father's passing, Nelson left his mother's kraal and was placed in **Chief Jongitaba Dalindyebo**'s household at **Mqhekezweni, the "Great Place"** to be a chief. Fanny passed away in 1968 while Nelson was in prison on Robben Island and he was not permitted to attend her funeral.

MANDELA, THEMBEKILE MADIBA (February 23, 1945–July 13, 1969). The eldest son of Nelson Mandela and **Evelyn Mase**, Thembekile Mandela was killed in a car accident near Touws River in the interior of the Western Cape. At the time of the death and funeral, Nelson was incarcerated on Robben Island and he was overwhelmed at the loss of his son, who carried the family clan name of Madiba as well as the nickname "Styles" for his dapper appearance. Refused permission to attend the funeral, Nelson struggled with his grief and tried in vain to hire a lawyer to gather information about the accident. Thembekile was survived by his wife Molly and their two children, Ndileka Mandela (born 1965) and Nandi Mandela (born 1968).

MANDELA UNITED FOOTBALL CLUB. Following her return in 1986 to **Soweto** after her banishment to Brantford, **Winnie Madikizela-Mandela** assembled the Mandela United Football Club (MUFC), a thuggish bodyguard ostensibly in the guise of a sports team football club (also known as soccer, a corruption of the historic term "association football" for the sport). Led by "coach" Jerry Vusi Richardson, the club became notorious for violence and brutal enforcement of Winnie's often wanton demands to police the townships of Soweto and punish those who informed on **African National Congress** (ANC) activists to state security. Richardson and other members of the club were

charged with the murder of fourteen-year-old Stompie Seipei, a youth activist accused by Winnie as a police informer. Richardson was also implicated in the killing of Dr. Abu-Bakr Asvat, a physician who had attended to Stompie's wounds inflicted by members of MFUC. Although Richardson often defended Winnie, whom he referred to as "Mummy," and shielded her from police investigations, at his trial for Stompie's murder, he claimed it was Winnie who had directed the torture and killing of dozens of "enemies." He was sentenced in 1991 to life in prison and died there of natural causes. Despite Nelson Mandela's repeated demands for her to disband the gang, Winnie persisted in deploying them to build the political base and to bully her detractors. Her daughter **Zindziswa Mandela-Hlongawne** had a child with one of the members of the MUFC and was often seen accompanying the team as a female mascot. She too was implicated in directing some of the violence, though she did not face prosecution. A judge, Chief Justice Michael Corbett, later reduced Winnie's sentence to a fine without jail time for her conviction on charges related to her role in MUFC kidnappings.

MASE-MANDELA-RAKEEPILE, EVELYN NTOKO (May 18, 1922–April 30, 2004). The first wife of Nelson Mandela, and mother of four children with him, Evelyn Mandela (née Mase) was born in Engcobo, Transkei to a father who was a mineworker, who passed away when she was an infant, and a mother who died when she was twelve. Evelyn then went to live with an elder brother, Sam, in **Johannesburg**, where she could attend school. At the time, Sam was living with **Walter** and **Albertina Sisulu**, close family friends and relations as Walter's mother and Evelyn's mother were related. Over the years, Evelyn remained close with the Sisulus and pursued a career in nursing, as Albertina had. It was at the Sisulus' home that she met Nelson. Smitten, he began to court her at the hospital in Hilbrow where she worked. They married soon thereafter in October 1944 just as Nelson was embarking on both his studies toward an LLB degree at the University of the Witwatersrand and becoming more deeply engaged in opposition politics with the **African**

National Congress (ANC) Youth League. In 1945, they had their first child, **Madiba Thembekile**, who would later die in a car crash. The first daughter, Makaziwe, was born in 1948 but she died in infancy at nine months old, and this was a heavy emotional blow to both parents. A son, **Makgatho Mandela**, born in 1950 survived into adulthood, but passed away from AIDS-related complications in 2005. A second daughter arrived in 1954, and they named her **Makaziwe Mandela** in memory of the first daughter. It was at this time that tensions in the marriage emerged. As Nelson's commitment to the ANC intensified, he was seemingly always busy with politics and rarely at home. When Evelyn went away to further her studies with a course on midwifery, it appeared that Nelson may have had an affair. Further stress came with state security police monitoring and harassing the family. Evelyn, a deeply devout person from her upbringing, then took the birth of a second daughter as a sign from god. She became involved with the Watchtower Movement, and soon converted to become a dedicated Jehovah's Witness. As she instructed the children in her newfound faith, Nelson poured himself deeper into politics, leading to estrangement. Once embroiled in the **Treason Trial** and often in jail, Nelson and Evelyn had effectively been separated. According to Evelyn, the relationship was under great strain and, on one occasion, she claimed Nelson physically assaulted her. Despite Evelyn's pleadings and interventions from the Sisulus and **Kaiser Matanzima**, when she presented him with an ultimatum to choose either the religion and family or the ANC, Nelson chose the latter and the couple divorced in 1958. Evelyn then moved back to the Transkei with the children and operated a small grocery store there for many years. She later returned to **Soweto** as a missionary, and met and married Simon Rakeepile, a local businessman and fellow devout Jehovah's Witness. Nelson Mandela as well as his two other wives, **Winnie Madikizela-Mandela** and **Graça Machel**, attended her funeral in 2004.

MATANZIMA, NKOSI (PARAMOUNT CHIEF) KAISER DALIWONGA (June 15, 1915–June 15, 2003).

Kaiser Matanzima, technically Nelson Mandela's nephew by **Thembu** custom, was his elder and fellow student at the **University of Fort Hare**, where he also studied law. Matanzima and Mandela were close friends, with Mandela serving as best man at his wedding, until their political paths diverged. Despite his strong criticism of the White-dominated state and the effects of apartheid, Matanzima sought personal political power through the new apparatus of the Bantu Authorities Act of 1951. In 1955, in a controversial move, Matanzima accepted a government appointment as paramount chief of the Emigrant Thembuland as part of a plan to develop separate "Bantustans" or African puppet states within South Africa. Having survived an assassination attempt by Black nationalists, Matanzima drew the ire of the ANC and Mandela for taking a leadership role in the semiautonomous Transkeian Territorial Authority, with Mandela referring to him as a sell-out and traitor to the liberation struggle. Following territorial elections in 1976, Mantanzima became prime minister of the "independent" Transkei, a state that was recognized only by, and totally dependent on, the South African government. He also authored *Independence My Way* to explain his case for emancipation through a federation of independent African states in South Africa. Thereafter, he took on the title of president, with his brother, George Matanzima, serving as prime minister. Together, they became notorious for a brutal and repressive regime and by 1986, the South African government forced both the Matanzimas from power for their excesses.

MBEKI, GOVAN ARCHIBALD MVUYELWA (July 9, 1910–August 30, 2001).

A leading figure in the **African National Congress** (ANC) and the South African Communist Party (SACP), Govan Mbeki was friend and comrade to Nelson Mandela through the long years of their imprisonment together on Robben Island. Govan was also the father, with his wife Epainatte, of **Thabo Mbeki**, the controversial figure who succeeded Mandela as president of South Africa in 1999, and three other children, Linda, Moeletsi, and Jama. Govan Mbeki was born and raised in the Transkei, not far from where

Mandela grew up. As with Mandela, Mbeki's father, Sikelewu Mbeki, was a chief who was deposed by the White colonial government, and Govan also studied at the **University of Fort Hare**, earning a bachelor's degree in 1936. The Mbekis were committed to helping the poor in their region and started food aid programs and a cooperative store to provide affordable goods. While there, he met and learned about opposition politics from various African leaders who were involved in the ANC and SACP. He joined the ANC in 1935 and was a member of the SACP by the end of the 1930s. A life-long journalist and writer, Mbeki penned a number of works that were important for struggling politics and academics, including his celebrated *The Peasant's Revolt* (1964), written on toilet paper and smuggled out of Robben Island, which analyzed various rural African opposition movements in South Africa. He also served as managing editor of the SACP's *New Age* magazine which was later banned by the state. Mbeki was among those members of the high command of **Umkhonto We Sizwe (MK)**, the armed wing of the ANC, who were caught in a police raid on July 11, 1963, on Liliesleaf Farm in Rivonia, **Johannesburg** and subsequently tried for conspiracy to overthrow the South African government by violent means. Following their conviction at the **Rivonia Trial**, Mbeki and Mandela, who was implicated in absentia (he was in prison serving a sentence on other charges at the time) for sabotage by papers found during the raid, served their sentences together in the harsh conditions on Robben Island. It was there that the two of them, along with other leaders, debated politics and contending approaches to the liberation struggle. As a diehard communist, Mbeki so opposed some of Mandela's views on economics and African nationalist ideals that he refused to speak with Mandela for a number of years while on the island. Mbeki was released in 1987 after serving twenty-four years in prison. He later served as a senator in the new ANC government until 1999, and he passed away in 2001.

MBEKI, THABO MVUYELWA (June 18, 1942–). Thabo Mbeki was the controversial second president, from 1999–2008, of a democratic South Africa following the end of Nelson Mandela's one and only term in the office. As part of the second generation of **African National Congress** (ANC) and South African Communist Party (SACP) leaders who had grown up with apartheid, Thabo's life and career were profoundly shaped by the struggle against apartheid. His father, **Govan Mbeki**, was a renowned member of the ANC and served twenty-four years in prison alongside Mandela, though the two did not always see eye-to-eye on the policy and theory of the party. Thabo's parents affirmed the value of Western education and so made considerable efforts to provide for his schooling at various Christian mission schools in their home area of Transkei including the prestigious Lovedale College. Established by Scottish Presbyterians in the 1840s, it was the first high-school-level institution in the country to admit Africans. Having been raised by a diehard Marxist-socialist, Mbeki embraced the far-Left politics of the opposition movements from an early age, and joined the ANC Youth League at the age of fourteen. He parents supported him moving to **Johannesburg** in the early 1960s, where he met Mandela just prior to his incarceration. By that time, South Africa was already embroiled in tension and state violence against opposition movements. The government had already banned the ANC and the SACP, driving some African leaders underground or out of the country, and others, such as Mandela, were facing various criminal charges for political opposition to the state. Having been groomed for leadership from an early age, Thabo was also sent out of the country to hone his skills and help develop the ANC's capacities. In 1962, he and over twenty other young members of the party left South Africa, traveling via neighboring Botswana to ANC training camps in Tanzania. Thabo carried on his voyage to join **Oliver Tambo** and the ANC leadership in exile in London. They then supported him to undertake studies at the University of Sussex where he eventually completed graduate-level work in economics and politics. From that time, Thabo was viewed by many in the rank-and-file of the ANC as somewhat effete, an image he could not shake even into his rise to popularity and the presidency. He, nevertheless, was keen to engage in more revolutionary strategy and tactics and was finally granted, in 1969, permission to receive military training in methods of insurgency and sabotage in the Soviet Union. Thereafter, Thabo rose through the ranks of the ANC leadership, joining the Revolutionary Council in exile in the early 1970s. He then returned to Africa, this time to Lusaka, Zambia, where the ANC leadership in exile south to orchestrate its insurgency from the frontline states including Swaziland and later, after its independence in 1980, Zimbabwe. Despite his work with training guerrilla insurgents while in Swaziland, Thabo's forte turned out to be more along the lines of public relations and diplomatic negotiations for the ANC. It was, for example, while in exile that Thabo liaised with ANC party member and homeland leader **Mangosuthu Buthelezi** about setting up the foundations of the Inkatha Freedom Party (IFP) such that it also could potentially serve as a base of opposition to the apartheid state. Then, from 1982, Thabo played a key role in paving the way to eventual negotiations with the apartheid government. He was appointed as chief of the ANC's Department of Information and Publicity and he helped raise international awareness of the oppression and suffering of Blacks in South Africa caused by apartheid. More significantly, he helped shape the ANC policy which emphasized the image and experience of both Nelson and **Winnie Mandela** as the representatives of the plight of political prisoners in particular and the ANC more generally. In 1986, while he was still out of the country, a team of South African state security forces bombed his home in exile in Lusaka in an apparent assassination attempt. Then, between 1987 and 1990, before Mandela's release, Thabo played a pivotal role in a team of ANC delegates who held a series of secret talks with members of the apartheid government as wells as leaders from the South African investment and business sector. He also played a leading role, alongside **Jacob Zuma**, in the negotiations leading to full democratic elections in 1994. After considerable internal political debate, Mandela selected Thabo as his first deputy president, with **F. W.**

de Klerk serving as the second in the **Government of National Unity** (GNU). During this time, Thabo further consolidated his support in the ANC, especially among members of the Youth League and the Women's League, and so was able to beat out both Zuma and **Cyril Ramaphosa** to lead the ANC and then succeed Mandela as the second president of an all-democratic South Africa. Despite launching the emotionally uplifting political platform of his "African Renaissance," Thabo was seen as a controversial president for several key reasons. First, he was mired in corruption charges for a dubious government arms deal that likely included kickbacks. More significantly for Mandela, Thabo emerged as an **HIV/AIDS** denialist who embraced decidedly unscientific arguments about the origins of the epidemic that was devastating the country during the 1990s. Thabo's approach became all the more embarrassing for Mandela after his son, **Makgatho Mandela**, died from AIDS-related complications in 2005. Thabo also felt compelled to dismiss Winnie Mandela from her government post following accusations of involvement in corruption. He then ran afoul of the increasingly popular Zuma when he also fired him from his post as deputy president, setting off a deep rift in the ANC that, combined with his apparent inability to address critical economic issues in the country, eventually led to Zuma taking over party leadership and the presidency. Despite his unease with Thabo's aloof academic style and troubling charges of corruption, Nelson Mandela, having served one term as president, stayed true to his commitment not to interfere with party politics once he stepped down, and so did not offer comment on Thabo's presidency.

MEER, FATIMA (August 12, 1928–March 12, 2010). Fatima Meer was an antiapartheid activist, academic, and friend of Nelson Mandela. Her *Higher Than Hope* (1990) was one of the first authorized biographies of Mandela, a testament to her activist credentials and closeness to him. Meer was the daughter of Moosa Meer, a Gujurati-born Indian who edited *Indian Views*, an anticolonial resistance newspaper for the Muslim-Indian community in Durban. She engaged in opposition from an early age, including the 1946 Indian Passive Resistance campaign. She embraced radical politics, followed Trotskyist ideals, and also cultivated her studies of Mohandas Gandhi's passive-resistance tactics while studying at the University of Natal, where she took an MA in sociology. In 1951, she married Ismail Meer, a fellow antiapartheid activist and together they became close friends of Mandela. Meer and her husband were tireless campaigners for Indian and African rights as well as for collaboration among all parts of oppressed Black society, for which she was repeatedly "banned" (legally constrained to not speak publicly or write against state policies or to associate with other activists) by the government. She was instrumental garnering attention and support for all the accused, including her husband Ismail and Mandela, during the **Treason Trial** and she worked closely with **Winnie Mandela** in the Black Women's Federation. She later declined to join Nelson Mandela's government as a member of parliament, preferring to remain outside party politics, though she served on his presidential advisory committee and many other civic organizations, and remained an active academic and writer until her death.

MLANGENI, ANDREW MOKETE (June 6, 1925–). Jailed for twenty-six years along with Nelson Mandela, Andrew Mlangeni was a codefendant in **Rivonia Trial**. Born and raised in **Soweto**, Mlangeni joined the **African National Congress** (ANC) Youth League in 1951 and became a full member of the ANC in 1955 when he served as a delegate from Kliptown to the **Congress of the People**. As with Mandela, and as part of the armed struggle and the work of **Umkhonto We Sizwe (MK)**, the ANC sent Mlangeni out of the country for military training in 1961. He was arrested upon his return in 1963, and imprisoned on Robben Island. After his release, he served as an ANC member of parliament in the new democratic government from 1994 to 1999. Mlangeni spoke eloquently at Mandela's memorial service in 2013, and also had a leading role in the documentary

about Mandela and the Rivonia Trial "Life Is Wonderful" (directed by Nick Stadlen, 2017).

MOTSAMAYI, DAVID. David Motsamayi was the pseudonym that Nelson Mandela used when he went underground following the banning of the **African National Congress** (ANC) in 1960. It was the name of a former client of Mandela's law practice. The surname *Motsamayi* translates as "the walker" and was intended as a tongue-in-cheek reference to his peripatetic efforts to avoid arrest. Mandela used this name on his forged passport when he went on his African tour in 1962. While in **Johannesburg**, Mandela had pretended to be the caretaker and cook at Liliesleaf Farm, Rivonia and was known to the secret police by this name and an arrest warrant was made out for "David Motsamayi, caretaker and cook" when the police raided the farm. In the event, Mandela was already in jail on other charges, having been caught based on a tip from an American Central Intelligence Agency operative as he chauffeured his White ally and member of the **Congress of Democrats** (COD) **Cecil Williams** while driving outside of Howick, KwaZulu-Natal.

MQHEKEZWENI, "THE GREAT PLACE." Nelson Mandela was introduced to the customs and practice of **Thembu** leadership and society at Mqhekezweni, "the Great Place" of **Chief Jongitaba Dalindyebo**. Following the death of his father **Nkosi (chief) Mphakanyiswa Henry Gadla Mandela**, Nelson's mother **Nonqaphi Nosekeni Mandela** was without the means to continue supporting her son's formal fee-based education, and so as his father had arranged, he moved into the regent Chief Jongitaba's household at Mqhekezweni. There, Mandela not only undertook range of household chores, including ironing the regent's pants, he also learned about chiefly authority in the context of Cape and British colonial indirect rule. Mandela was also expected to regularly attend services at the Wesleyan Methodist missionary church, which had been established in 1820 under the auspices of a large wave of British Methodist immigrants to the Eastern

Cape. The African ministers and educated lay members of the church impressed Mandela with their formal Western education and trappings of British culture to the extent he further embraced his missionary education opportunities. It was also at Mqhekezweni, at the age of sixteen, that Mandela underwent *abakhwetha*, the ritual circumcision and related training that marked male **Xhosa** and Thembu youths' passage into "manhood."

N

NELSON MANDELA AWARD FOR HEALTH
AND HUMAN RIGHTS. This award was
established in 1992 at the behest of Nelson
Mandela by the Henry J. Kaiser Family Foundation (KFF), a nonprofit global public-health
research foundation that had been working in
South Africa, to recognize people who make
extraordinary contributions to improving the
health and health care of South Africans who
are among the most disadvantaged in society. Mandela, and later the Nelson Mandela
Foundation, worked with KFF to nominate
awardees, and past recipients have included
a number of people and organizations fighting
to combat the **HIV/AIDS** epidemic such as the
Treatment Action Campaign.

Nelson Mandela. *Courtesy of the Nelson Mandela Foundation.*

R

RAMAPHOSA, CYRIL MATAMELA (November 17, 1952–). The fifth president (since 2018) of a democratic South Africa, Cyril Ramaphosa was widely reputed to be Nelson Mandela's choice to succeed him as president. Ramaphosa played a pivotal role in the negotiations for a democratic transition. Born in **Soweto, Johannesburg**, Ramaphosa was a staunch opponent of apartheid as he worked through the ranks of the activist Black South African Student Organization and then the trade union movement. He undertook legal studies through the University of South Africa and became active as legal counsel and then labor union organizer for the National Union of Mineworkers, an affiliate of the South African Congress of Trade Unions (SACTU), which is part of the antiapartheid Tripartite Alliance with the South African Communist Party and the **African National Congress** (ANC). With his solid trade-union credentials, he easily won election as General Secretary of the ANC in 1991 after he helped in the negotiations that paved the way for Mandela's release from prison. Ramaphosa also rose to prominence and some considerable fortune as a successful businessman, and despite some criticism from those on the far left, he has never been associated with corruption the same way as other ANC leaders have been. Despite Mandela's backing, he still lost out on the popular vote that led to **Thabo Mbeki**'s presidency. He then served as deputy president under **Jacob Zuma** from 2014 until 2018.

RESHA, ROBERT (March 9, 1920–December 7, 1973). Robert Resha was a member of the **African National Congress** (ANC) Youth League with Nelson Mandela, and later joined the organization's executive committee. An activist from an early age, Resha was involved in the **Defiance Campaign** in 1952, and was one of the 156 accused in the **Treason Trial** in 1956. He was a well-known journalist and wrote extensively for the *New Age*, the South African Communist Party (SACP) news magazine. While charges were dismissed against most of the defendants in that trial, Resha and Mandela were among those not acquitted until 1961. Resha was among a select number of ANC members who accompanied Mandela along the way on **Mandela's Africa tour** in 1962. The two worked together and received military training in Algeria as part of the tour. Thereafter, Resha remained out of South Africa in exile and died in London.

RIVONIA TRIAL (October 9, 1963–June 12, 1964). The Rivonia Trial was perhaps the single most important event in Nelson Mandela's political life prior to his election to president of South Africa in the first fully democratic election in 1994. The court proceedings and international press coverage associated with the trial revealed both the commitment of members of the **African National Congress**'s (ANC) armed wing, **Umkhonto We Sizwe (MK)**, to the liberation struggle and the White government's resolve to break it. It also brought into clear relief, through one of the world's most iconic speeches, the character and courage of Nelson Mandela, for it was at this trial that he delivered the now famous lines, "During my lifetime I have dedicated myself to this struggle of the African people. I have fought against White domination, and I have fought against Black domination. I have cherished the ideal of a democratic and free society in which all persons live together in harmony and with equal opportunities. It is an ideal which I hope to live for and to achieve. But if needs be, it is an ideal for which I am prepared to die." Curiously, the trial had its origins at Liliesleaf Farm, which had been purchased in South African Communist Party (SCAP) member Arthur Goldreich's name, in Rivonia which was, in 1963, on the fringes of **Johannesburg** and Mandela was not even there at the time. Although Mandela had frequented the farm in the guise of his undercover identity "David Motsamyi" (isiXhosa for David "the walker" and a play on his many peregrinations to elude the police), he was already serving a sentence in the prison on Robben Island when security police raided the premises and arrested eleven members of the MK High Command and the SACP. They had been gathering there for over two years to work on, among other things, Operation Mayibuye (isiXhosa and isiZulu for "Comeback"), which was widely acknowledged by members of MK and the ANC to have been mostly an impractical aspirational plan for combined mass resistance, military operations, and sabotage, and they had stored various planning documents on the farm, documents which also implicated Mandela. As a result, Mandela was brought up to the Pretoria High Court and charged along with **Lionel "Rusty" Bernstein**; **Denis Goldberg**, leader of the **Congress of Democrats** (COD); Arthur Goldreich, owner of Liliesleaf Farm; Bob Hepple; James Kantor; **Ahmed Kathrada**; **Govan Mbeki**; Raymond Mhlaba; Andrew Mlangeni; Elias Motsoaledi; **Walter Sisulu**, secretary-general of the ANC; and the academic, Harold Wolpe. Wolpe and Goldreich bribed a guard and managed to escape from the Pretoria jail to then flee into exile in the United Kingdom. The rest faced a most serious set of charges including over two hundred acts of sabotage and fomenting revolution and for which the highest penalty was the death sentence. It was also at this time that the state connected **Mandela's Africa tour** to his efforts to train and raise funds for the resistance. Among the gifted defense team of lawyers were **Bram Fischer**, **Joel Joffe**, and **George Bizos**, who became a life-long friend and counsel to the Mandela family. Their work, as well as searing international scrutiny of the trial driven by the international antiapartheid movement as well as condemnation from the United Nations, helped the defendants avoid the death penalty. Eight of them, Mandela included, however, were sentenced to life in prison. Consistent with the perverse logic of apartheid, the convicted Black defendants were sent to Robben Island while White defendants were segregated out to Pretoria Central Prison.

S

SIDELSKY, LAZAAR (October 7, 1911–May 17, 2002). Lazar Sidelsky, the son of Jewish Lithuanian refugees to South Africa, was a partner in the **Johannesburg** law firm of Witkin, Sidelsky and Eidelman. Sidelsky and the firm took a progressive antiapartheid stance, and hired Africans to work in the firm and to assist poor Black clients. While there, Nelson Mandela befriended another White lawyer, Nat Bregman, who invited Nelson to "mixed parties" where Whites and Blacks socialized and introduced him to fellow members of the Communist Party of South Africa (CPSA). On the advice of **Walter Sisulu**, who had been a client of the firm, Sidelsky hired and mentored Mandela, waiving the usual clerking fees so the young aspiring lawyer could complete law school and start his articles, which he later completed at the firm of Terblanche and Briggish. Sidelsky also loaned him £50 and gave him an old suit. Sidelsky, who admonished Mandela not to get involved in politics, maintained their friendship, and later visited him in prison.

SISULU, ALBERTINA NONTSIKELELO (October 21, 1918–June 2, 2011). Affectionately known a "Ma Sisulu" and "Mother of the Nation," Albertina Sisulu (née Thethiwe) joined the **African National Congress** (ANC) and opposition politics later in life, after marrying **Walter Sisulu**. She then helped advise and lead the organization, especially during challenging times when male leaders were banned or imprisoned. Born in Camama village in Tsomo district of the Transkei, from eleven years old Albertina had to help raise her three siblings after her father, a miner, died and because her mother's health had been compromised by influenza during the worldwide pandemic of 1918. Despite setbacks in Presbyterian mission schools, she excelled in academics and sports while a scholarship student at the Catholic Mariazell College in Matatilele in the Eastern Cape. Although she aspired to become a nun, she realized that calling would not provide the means her family needed so, after graduation in 1940, she traveled to **Johannesburg** to begin a career in nursing at what was then the "non-European" section of Johannesburg General Hospital (now Charlotte Maxeke Johannesburg Academic General Hospital). It was while there that she met and became friends with **Evelyn Mase**, who was later to become Nelson Mandela's wife, and also Rosabella "Barbie" Sisulu, her future husband's sister. It was among these and the other still small number of women who had migrated to urban jobs in the early years of apartheid that she became aware of the racial oppression in the country. This experience made her more open to socializing with other political activists in the city and how she came to meet and then marry Walter Sisulu.

Albertina wed Walter Sisulu at the Bantu Men's Social Club in Johannesburg in 1944 with Mandela serving as best man, along with Evelyn Mase and Anton Lemebe in the wedding party. Thereafter, the Sisulu family grew apace as the couple had five of their own children, including **Zwelakhe Sisulu**, and then adopted four more. Walter and his friends were already very politically active, having joined the ANC and helped to establish the ANC Youth League (ANCYL). Albertina was, however, initially hesitant to join the ANC, in part because it appeared to her to be a largely all-male organization. The ANC only accepted women members from 1943, and she was, after all, the only woman in attendance at the 1944 ANCYL conference. She was, nevertheless, swept up into the organization as her husband's commitment to it intensified. From their home in the Orlando West section of **Soweto**, the Sisulus served in various leadership roles in the antiapartheid movement. In 1947, Walter left his regular job in real estate to work full time for the ANC, and the family had to rely on Albertina's modest nurse's salary. While she went on to qualify as a midwife for better pay, she became increasingly involved in the women's movement in the antiapartheid struggle, including the recently formed Federation of South African Women (FEDSAW). In 1955, she joined the ANC Women's League (ANCWL) executive and then helped lead in 1956, along with Helen Joseph and others, the twenty-thousand-person strong women's protest march against pass laws to the Union Government buildings in Pretoria, the national administrative, and executive capital. In 1963, their children became, effectively, orphaned for a time as both Walter and Albertina were jailed. Albertina was the first women held under a ninety-day detention order under sweeping General Laws Amendment Act aimed at any political opponent of the state. She faced numerous other detentions and bans as a political activist over the next twenty years, and, after Walter was sentenced to life in prison on Robben Island with Mandela, her children too were subjected state security harassment. As the number of informants that the state police recruited in the townships increased, Albertina had to devise inventive methods of communicating with ANC allies through the thin walls of her home and adjoining homes. She nevertheless continued her work with the ANC, including arranging for young activists to flee the country to attend training camps in various other African countries. By the 1980s, South Africa was in violent turmoil. Most opposition political parties, including the ANC, had been

banned and had to operate either from exile or under the guise of reconstituted organizations. Fortunately, although she had suffered as a banned person for over eighteen years, the longest of any person in the country, Albertina's banning order was not renewed by the state in 1981, allowing her to take part in public gathering and political activity. In 1983, the United Democratic Front (UDF) took on the role of leading a broad vanguard of civic, church, and political organizations, including an informal representation of underground elements of the ANC (though not with the armed resistance) in opposition to the state. Albertina was elected one of three copresidents, along with Archie Gumede and Oscar Mpetha.

By the later 1980s, Albertina had become a key symbolic figure, "Ma," an honorific title reflecting her role as "mother of the nation." She was, however, challenged in that role by the more aggressive tactics of **Winnie Madikizela-Mandela**. Although she never publicly condemned her for the sake of the party, Albertina was personally horrified at Winnie's corrupt and criminal behavior in aid of the cause. Albertina worked for Dr. Abu Bakr Asvat in the Soweto clinic when Winnie had brought in two female youth to be examined for signs of sexual assault. When Asvat could find no signs to help justify Winnie's role in punishing those she alleged had committed the assault, Winnie was furious. He was murdered a few days later by members of the **Mandela United Football Club** (MUFC). Though she suspected Winnie's direct involvement, Albertina never spoke against her on the charge, even before the Truth and Reconciliation Commission (TRC). Following her husband's release from prison in 1989, the Sisulus enjoyed leading roles in the new government. Albertina served as an ANC member of parliament and a leading figure in the ANCWL as well as the FEDSAW. In July of 1994, along with over a thousand guests, they celebrated their fiftieth wedding anniversary. Albertina grieved the loss of her husband Walter in 2003, and retreated from public life until her passing in 2011. Their children went on to leading roles in service of the ANC government, including as ambassadors and ministers.

**SISULU, WALTER MAX ULYATE XHAMELA
(May 18, 1912–May 5, 2003).** Walter Sisulu was a South African antiapartheid activist, member of the **African National Congress** (ANC), close friend and mentor to Nelson Mandela and cofounder with him, Anton Lembede, and others of the ANC Youth League (ANCYL). Sometimes referred to as "Mandela's aide," Sisulu played a more significant role in shaping ANC policy than this sobriquet might suggest. He was more reverentially known as Tata (father) Sisulu or by his **Xhosa** clan name, Xhamela. Sisulu was born in Qutubeni, near Ngcobo in the same region of the Transkei that Mandela hailed from though from a very different family background. His mother, Alice Mase Sisulu, who was related to Mandela's first wife **Evelyn Mase**, was a domestic worker in the White government municipal offices in nearby Umtata where she met Albert Dickenson, a White assistant magistrate and railway company employee. Their relationship was considered unacceptable and Dickinson estranged himself from the family. Although common, such liaisons across racial lines were outlawed in South Africa under the Immorality Act (1927 and 1950) and the Prohibition of Mixed Marriages Act, 1949. This left Sisulu to be born outside of a marriage and, technically speaking under the laws of apartheid, classified as "Coloured," an official designation for people of mixed race. Dickenson took little part in raising his child and Sisulu was raised by an uncle and a grandmother. His early education at an Anglican mission school was cut short when his uncle died in 1926, and at the age of fifteen he was compelled to leave for search of work to help support the family, eventually leading him to **Johannesburg**. There he worked variously as a laborer in the mines, as a domestic worker, and at a bakery from which he was fired for instigating a strike. During this period he also returned to the Transkei to further his education and undergo the customary Xhosa initiation ceremonies marking his entry to manhood, just as Mandela had done. He also sojourned in East London where he met and was influenced by Clements Kadalie, the famous leader of the Industrial and Commercial Workers Union of South Africa, a self-help labor organization for Africans in the Eastern Cape region.

By the 1940s, Sisulu had settled in Johannesburg and become more politically active. After working with a White real estate agent for a time, he established his own agency to assist Blacks in purchasing and leasing homes and property in the city. Sitha Investments was, at the time, the only Black-owned real estate agency in the country. The company offices also became the site of many visits from young intellectuals of the ANC such as Mandela and **Oliver Tambo**, who sought out Sisulu's wisdom and experience with the trade union movement. He also joined the ANC and became an active member in the South African Communist Party (SACP, banned by the government in 1950 and renamed as the Communist Party of South Africa [CPSA] in 1953). It was at this time that he welcomed the younger Mandela into his home and friendship, and then encouraged him to join the ANC. Sisulu also introduced Mandela to the White lawyer, **Lazar Sidelsky**. Sidelsky had done some legal work for Sisulu and so agreed to take Mandela on as an articled clerk so he could begin his legal career. Their friendship grew over the years to the extent that, in 1944, Mandela served as best man to Walter and his bride **Albertina Sisulu** (née Thethiwe) at their wedding in the Transkei. Together, they had five children and adopted four others, most of whom also became active in opposition politics. Their son **Zwelakhe Sisulu** later also served as a journalist and press secretary to Mandela when he was president. The Sisulus also introduced Mandela to his first wife, Evelyn, who was a nurse as was Albertina, although, influenced by Walter, Albertina embraced political activism while Evelyn eschewed it in favor of her faith.

Walter Sisulu's political activism led him to the top ranks of the ANC. Along with Mandela, Tambo, and Anton Lembede, Sisulu helped found the ANC Youth League (ANCYL) in 1944 as part of a vanguard of more radical members seeking to pressure the old guard leadership into stronger protests against the racial oppression of the government. In addition to helping found the ANCYL, he was elected secretary general of party in 1949. His radicalism, moreover, was a driving force in the ANC forging the Congress Alliance with the South African Indian Congress (SAIC) and Cape Franchise Action Committee, which represented Coloured voters. By 1952, Sisulu had been jailed and banned a number of times for his opposition to apartheid and his leadership on the **Defiance Campaign**. In 1953, he was among the 156 coaccused in the **Treason Trial**, which dragged on until all were eventually acquitted by 1961. As state repression intensified through the 1950s, Sisulu, Mandela, and other leaders stepped up their activities. He agreed with Mandela about the need for more assertive action, which was outlined in the M-Plan, named for Mandela's initial. Then, in 1953, after consultation with Mandela, Sisulu arranged with communist party members for him to travel first to a conference in Bucharest, Romania and then to the Soviet Union and on to China, where he asked for support and aid in the form of weapons to take up armed resistance. The Chinese, though supportive of the cause, did not provide arms, advising that such a move was premature and dangerous, and Sisulu returned to South Africa disappointed. More critically, he was instrumental in the decision, along with Mandela, **Joe Slovo** of the SACP and **Govan Mbeki**, to undertake the armed struggle and found **Umkhonto we Sizwe (Spear of the Nation or MK)**, the armed wing of the party. Having skipped bail for a court appearance on charges of furthering the aims of the banned ANC, Sisulu went underground, as Mandela had, to escape further police harassment. Then, on June 26, 1963, Sisulu made speech broadcast from a clandestine ANC radio station called Radio Liberation, which was housed at the organization's secret hideout, Liliesleaf Farm in Rivonia. Less than a month later the police raided the farm and he was arrested with Govan Mbeki, Raymond Mhlaba, **Ahmed Kathrada**, and others. Convicted in the infamous **Rivonia Trial**, the state sentenced Sisulu to life in prison for conspiring to commit sabotage.

Despite his incarceration on Robben Island, along with Mandela and other ANC leaders, Sisulu was able to masterfully orchestrate the ANC's secret campaign of resistance. Just as Tambo managed the external wing of the party, Sisulu developed an internal network referred to as the "High Organ" to help coordinate the clandestine campaign of resistance among those in prison. His wife Albertina acted as the liaison to their supporters across the country. Moreover Sisulu, along with others such as Mandela, Kathrada, and **Mac Maharaj**, helped transform the Robben Island Prison into the "university" for political prisoners by setting up and teaching courses on politics and African history. Referred to as "Syllabus A," the program included classes taught regularly at the island limestone quarry, where political prisoners were compelled to do hard labor. Mandela, among many other inmates, valued Sisulu's efforts to educate ANC and Pan African Congress (PAC) supporters who had little or no knowledge of their own political history. After enduring twenty-six years in prison, Sisulu was among a group of key members of the ANC that Mandela insisted be released as a precondition of him entering into talks about a negotiated settlement to end apartheid.

In October of 1989, Sisulu and other fellow prisoners from the Rivonia Trial were freed as a prelude to the release of Mandela, the unbanning of the ANC, and other opposition political parties and negotiations with the National Party (NP) government. In December of the next year, Sisulu was part of the ANC's national executive delegation that met in Cape Town with the government to begin negotiations for political transformation of the country. When the ANC held its first national conference inside South Africa since it was banned, the party elected Sisulu as deputy president. He served in that office until ill health forced him to retire from politics in 1994. He and his wife retired to Johannesburg where they engaged in charity work until Walter passed away in 2003.

SISULU, ZWELAKHE (December 17, 1950–October 4, 2012). Son of **Walter** and **Albertina Sisulu**, was a journalist and antiapartheid activist. From a young age, he witnessed firsthand the intensifying repression of the apartheid government when his father was sentenced to life in prison for opposing the state's racist laws. He began reporting on state repression for various newspapers soon after graduation from Orlando High School in **Soweto**. Over the years, the police harassed and arrested Zwelakhe many times for reporting on the use of violence and repression against political activists and for refusing to reveal his sources. He went on to found the ANC-aligned *New Nation* newspaper, which operated from 1986 until 1997 and had the largest circulation of any Black South African papers at the time. He also served as President Nelson Mandela's press secretary and chief information officer for the ANC and was later rewarded by the ANC government in 1994 with an appointment as director of the South African Broadcasting Corporation.

SLOVO, JOE YOSSEL MASHEL (May 3, 1926–January 6, 1995). Born in Lithuania, Joe Slovo was a leading member of the South African Communist Party (SACP) and cofounder with Nelson Mandela and commander of the **African National Congress** (ANC) armed wing, **Umkhonto We Sizwe (MK)**. Slovo's family moved to South Africa when he was eight years old and struggled as working-class Whites. Committed to the communist cause from an early age, he volunteered to serve in World War II fighting fascism in North Africa and Italy and wrote on the challenges of Stalinism for international communism. On his return, he studied law at the University of the Witwatersrand where he was a classmate of Mandela's. In 1949, he married fellow communist and antiapartheid activist Ruth First, who was later assassinated by South African security forces in 1982. Life for Slovo became increasingly difficult after the banning of the SACP in 1950. When Mandela was arrested near Howick, after his return from his **Africa tour** in 1962, Slovo assisted him in preparing his legal defense and his famous presentation, thus drawing further attention to Slovo for his work in opposition to apartheid.

By 1963, after a series of personal bannings, he went to live in exile the United Kingdom, Zambia, and Mozambique until the unbanning of opposition parties in 1990, when he returned to South Africa. Slovo was noted for his keen legal mind and understanding of politics and he made important contributions to both SACP and ANC policies. He played a pivotal role in saving the negotiations for a democratic South Africa by proposing the so-called sunset clause that allowed National Party (NP) government officials to share in a transitional **Government of National Unity** (GNU) for five years. Slovo served in the difficult post of minister of housing under President Mandela from 1994 until his death in 1995. Mandela praised Slovo at his funeral for his courage and commitment to fighting for the working class of South Africa, Black and White.

SOWETO. The "South West Township" or Soweto, was established in the 1930s by the all-White government under the auspices of the segregationist Natives (Urban Areas) Act (Act No. 21 of 1923) legislation as an agglomeration of various Black-only farms, townships, and informal shack settlements then outside of the city of **Johannesburg.** The name became synonymous with the liberation struggle of Blacks as the center of passive-resistance campaigns, many of which Nelson Mandela participated in or orchestrated. More infamously, it was the site of the Soweto Uprising of 1976, in which government police shot and killed African students and some twenty-three people died. Mandela and his family lived in the township at 8115 Vilakazi Street from the 1940s into the 1960s. Although he planned to live there after his release from prison, he left the house after a few weeks, and it was later turned over to the Soweto Heritage Trust to become the Nelson Mandela National Museum. Many other prominent members of the **African National Congress** (ANC) and later Mass Democratic Movement also lived, at one time or another, in Soweto.

T

TAMBO, ADELAIDE FRANCES (July 18, 1929–January 31, 2007). Deeply committed to the liberation struggle from an early age, "Mama Tambo" as she was affectionately known, was a dedicated nurse, devoted wife (née Tshukudu) to **African National Congress** (ANC) leader, **Oliver Tambo**, and friend to the Mandelas. Born in the African Top Location in the town of Vereeniging in the Transvaal, as she grew up Adelaide witnessed firsthand the brutalities of racism and state repression. She noted later in life that one incident in particular set her mind to take up opposition to the state and its repression. When a local police officer had been killed during protest riots in the location, her eighty-two-year-old grandfather was swept up by police and brought to the town square for failure to produce the government-issued pass required of all Africans. Although he had no role in the events, the police brutalized the older man alongside other Africans, and he collapsed while Adelaide sought to comfort him. She then vowed to fight against such injustice by joining the ANC.

Adelaide went through school in the Transvaal just as the government of Dr. Daniel Malan implemented formal apartheid policies. Her interest in the resistance movement led her to begin work at the age of fifteen for the local ANC chapter as a courier. By the age of eighteen, she had joined the ANC Youth League and was elected as the chairperson of the local **Johannesburg** chapter and became increasingly involved in political activism. Adelaide also built a career in nursing, training and working at the Pretoria General Hospital for a few years before moving to Baragwanath Hospital (now Chris Hani Baragwanath Hospital) in **Soweto**, reputed to be the largest hospital in the southern hemisphere.

Adelaide continued with her political activism during the tumultuous 1950s. In 1956, she, along with **Albertina Sisulu**, Helen Joseph, and others, was part of the twenty-thousand-strong march to the capital in Pretoria to protest against the extension of the hated pass laws to women. She also met her soon-to-be husband Oliver at a local ANC meeting. The two planned to marry and start a family, but she was compelled to make drastic changes when Oliver was arrested and charged in the infamous **Treason Trial**. The two were, nevertheless, married during the trial while Oliver, who was by then a member of the ANC executive, was out on bail. Over the next few years, as the trial dragged on, the Tambos had three children, Dali, Tembi, and Tselane. All the while, Adelaide remained supportive of Oliver and active with the ANC, providing a significant impetus for the development of the ANC's Women's League (ANCWL). When the state eventually dropped the charges against Oliver and many others for lack of foundation, and following the atrocity of the Sharpeville Massacre in 1960, the ANC executive decided to send the Tambos out of the country to establish and operate the wing of the organization in exile.

In 1960, following Oliver's departure, Adelaide and family joined him and settled in Muswell Hill, London. From their home there, the Tambos orchestrated a wide range of logistical and public relations activities for the ANC in exile. Adelaide hosted numerous ANC members who were exiled or out of South Africa on training missions. As Oliver spent much of his time traveling and lobbying on behalf of the ANC, it was up to Adelaide to maintain the home, raise the children and work as a nurse to support the family financially. In addition to this work, she also helped with the development of the international antiapartheid movement centered in London where she befriended Canon **John Collins** and Bishop Trevor Huddleston, both supporters of the movement. Moreover she became a founding member of the Afro-Asian Solidarity Movement, which supported self-determination and solidarity among developing member states. She also helped found the Pan African Women's organization in 1963.

After over thirty years in exile, the Tambos returned to South Africa following the unbanning of the ANC in 1990. Although by then, Oliver was in very poor health having suffered a severe stroke, the Tambos still played important roles in the lead up to the democratic transition of the country. Adelaide was elected in 1994 as an ANC member of parliament in the first nonracial government. Having lost her husband, who passed away in 1993, she served only one term in parliament but continued to play a leading role in the ANCWL. Indeed, despite a long-standing friendship with **Winnie Mandela** (she had introduced Nelson to her), Adelaide resigned from the executive of the ANCWL in protest over Winnie's leadership and her apparent fraud and misuse of organization funds. She continued to champion rights for the elderly until she died in 2007. Presidents Mandela, **Thabo Mbeki**, and Kenneth Kaunda of Zambia all attended her state funeral.

TAMBO, OLIVER REGINALD KAIZANA (October 27, 1917–April 24, 1993).

More affectionately known among members of the **African National Congress** (ANC) simply as O. R., Oliver Tambo was a friend and mentor to Nelson Mandela as well as a key antiapartheid politician and revolutionary. Having been a key founding member of the ANC Youth League (ANCYL) following the death of **Chief Albert Luthuli**, the then-president, Tambo served as president of the ANC from 1967 to 1991, although he had to do so from London while in exile since the state had banned the organization. He was among Mandela's closest and oldest friends since college days.

Born in Bizana in Pondoland, a region of the Transkei well known for its staunch opposition to British colonial rule and apartheid, Oliver's parents, Julia and Mzimeni Tambo, gave him the middle name of Kaizana (a vernacular form of "Kaiser") in honor of the German Kaiser Wilhelm for his opposition to the British in World War I. Though Mzimeni followed amaPondo customary practices and was polygamous, he later converted to Christianity and became as devout as Oliver's mother, Julia. They both affirmed the value of Western education and sought to place Oliver in various Christian mission schools, including the Ludeke Methodist school and then the more prestigious Anglican Holy Cross Mission school at Flagstaff. It was there that he was baptized into the Anglican faith and also developed his life-long love for music. Oliver Tambo engaged in the same sorts of activities that Mandela and most young men in the region followed such as herding cattle for their fathers, hunting birds and play stick-fighting, a common martial art among African youth, although, unlike Mandela, he bore scarification marks on his cheeks, a legacy of his coming-of-age rituals. As with Mandela, Tambo excelled in his studies, winning scholarships that enabled him to transfer to St. Peter's Anglican school in **Johannesburg**, from which he graduated. In 1941, Tambo attended the prestigious **University of Fort Hare** where he studied math and science and first met Nelson as part of the Student Christian Association activities. Tambo combined his strict Christian faith with political activism, eventually getting elected as president of the Student Representative Council (SRC). It was in that role that he led student protests against SRC electoral procedures and was expelled before he could complete the extended honors portion of his degree. He nevertheless earned the basic degree and went on to teach math at his alma mater, St. Peter's in Johannesburg.

From 1942, Tambo embarked on what would become among the most distinguished political careers within the ANC. While in Johannesburg, he again met up with Mandela through their mutual friend and supporter, the businessman and real estate agent, **Walter Sisulu**. Along with other politically minded opponents of segregation and the South African state, together they forged close ties with senior leaders of the ANC such as Dr. Alfred Xuma, the president of the ANC. These young men, however, remained disenchanted with the more cautious, conservative approach of the old guard in the ANC and so pressed for more active protests and nonviolent resistance. In support of this, Tambo, Mandela, and others drafted what would become the **Freedom Charter**, and then set about founding, in 1944, the ANCYL to represent a more radical and dynamic force within the ANC. Anton Lembede and Ashby Peter (AP) Mda were elected president and vice president respectively. Tambo was elected secretary and he took on responsibility for drafting many of the party's policy documents, including the Program of Action. Following the National Party (NP) election victory in 1948 and the full articulation of apartheid as government policy, Tambo, Mandela, and the ANC leadership faced even greater threats from state security. In 1953, when the ANC elected Luthuli as president, Tambo was appointed national secretary in place of Sisulu, who had recently been banned for his work on the **Defiance Campaign**. It was in that role that Tambo took on a more public profile in the antiapartheid movement, including helping arrange, with his spiritual mentor Father Trevor Huddleston, the visit from England of Canon **John Lewis Collins** aimed at gaining international recognition for the liberation struggle. The following year, Tambo's work on founding the **Congress of the People** and as the newly elected secretary general of the ANC led to his banning. From that point on, his life was bound and shaped entirely by his political activism.

Tambo was also well known for his work as a lawyer and partner with Nelson in the firm of Mandela and Tambo. His friendship with Sisulu had led to the two working on occasional legal matters, and Tambo had a comprehensive knowledge of customary or "traditional" African law relating to property and land rights. Tambo then pursued his articles as a law clerk with the White firm of Kramer and Tuch before he went to work for Solomon Kowalsky while studying for his law degree by correspondence, as almost all aspiring African lawyers had to, through the University of South Africa. Having met again in Johannesburg, his friend from his University of Fort Hare days, Nelson Mandela, came to admire Tambo's intellect and soft-spoken but powerful style. The two resolved, in 1952, to share a law practice, renting offices in Chancellor House in the center of the city, while continuing with their passionate work for the ANC cause. The firm of Mandela and Tambo was the first Black attorneys' practice in the country and it took on a wide range of African clientele faced with the increasing array of pernicious apartheid laws and restrictions on rights of residence and land purchase. In keeping with local practice, Tambo drafted most of the legal arguments and documents while the more flamboyant and outspoken Mandela presented the cases in court as the advocate. The firm grew and remained open for eight years until 1960, adding other African lawyers along the way including Duma Nokwe, Ruth Mompati, Mendi Msimang, and Godfrey Pitje. Mandela and Tambo, however, struggled to juggle politics and work at the firm, especially when they were both charged and caught up in the **Treason Trial** in 1956.

Over the next decade, Tambo rose to the key leadership role of the ANC in a context of increasing state repression. In 1956, the state charged Tambo along with Mandela, Luthuli, and 152 others with treason. As the Treason Trial opened, Tambo had also become engaged to his future wife, **Adelaide Tambo** (née Tshukudu), a nurse at Baragwanath hospital in Johannesburg who had been a member of the ANC since she was eighteen years of age. The wedding, planned for December of that year, almost did not happen as Tambo and others faced potential life sentences. He and Luthuli, however, were acquitted early on in the trial, and his marriage took place after all. Yet government harassment continued unabated, and he was left to manage the law practice while Mandela was still on trial for treason. When, in 1957, Tambo was elected vice president of the ANC, he and his family faced even greater challenges. First, in 1958 when Tambo served as chair of the annual ANC conference, he was confronted by strong challenges from a faction of staunch Africanists who rejected White and communist influences in the party. Although Tambo managed to ease tensions at the conference, the faction nevertheless later split away to form the Pan African Congress (PAC) under the leadership of Robert Sobukwe. In 1959, Tambo headed the ANC's constitutional commission, which came to be known as the Tambo Commission. It recommended greater recognition for the ANC's Women's League (ANCWL) and the ANCYL, and endorsed multiracialism and the Freedom Charter in place of the Program of Action. Following the devastating blow of the Sharpeville Massacre in March of 1960, the ANC executive decided that the organization needed create a diplomatic leadership structure that could operate unfettered from outside the country. Accordingly, Oliver and Adelaide Tambo and their three children left South Africa for London, England, where he was to operate in exile to support the ANC and gain international support for the antiapartheid movement. From their London home, Tambo and his wife welcomed and supported many ANC operatives in exile over the years, promoted the profile of the struggle, and more importantly, raised considerable sums of money to support the cause. Moreover he traveled extensively in support of the ANC mission, including in 1961 to accompany Luthuli to Stockholm to receive the Nobel Peace Prize. In 1962, he met with Mandela in Dar es Salaam, Tanzania (then Tanganyika) to discuss the formation of **Umkhonto We Sizwe (MK)** and then joined him on parts of his **African tour** for training and diplomacy. Tambo also made trips to China and the USSR as well as to New York in October of 1963 to address the United Nations about the repression of apartheid. Internal political tensions over democratic procedures within the ANC led to an attempt to force Tambo out

of the leadership, but in 1967 at the Morogoro conference in Tanzania, the party's first ever outside of South Africa, he was reelected president and he remained in the leadership in exile until his return to South Africa. In the intervening years, he developed a range of strategies to increase the pressure internally and externally on the White regime in power. Among the key efforts were greater support for the exiled components of the ANC and pressure against the apartheid regime from the "frontline" states that bordered South Africa such as newly independent Zimbabwe, Botswana, and even Lesotho, the mountainous kingdom entirely landlocked by South Africa. In 1982, in retaliation for these activities, the South African Defence Force (SADF) retaliated against ANC operatives in various states, including the killing of forty-two people in Maseru, the capital of Lesotho. In an almost miraculous effort, Tambo was able to travel to and make a surprise appearance at the funerals of the fallen comrades, giving a significant public relations boost to the party in a time of grief. Further controversial actions by Tambo revealed the escalating stakes in the fight against apartheid. Among these were Tambo's decision, in May of 1983 and in the face of SADF reprisals, to intensify the armed struggle by authorizing **Joe Slovo**, then head of MK, to execute the Church Street car bombing. Intended to target the South African Air Force headquarters in the national capital, Pretoria, the explosion set off at the height of rush hour killed nineteen people, including the two bombers, and wounded over two hundred others, causing international opprobrium. Additionally, pressures in ANC training camps across Africa had led to questionable practices intended to ferret out and punish government spies and collaborators among the ANC trainees. In a number of cases, these practices included torture and murder. Despite Tambo's condemnation of these practices and the infamous use of "necklacing" espoused by **Winnie Madikizel-Mandela** among others, Tambo, Nelson Mandela, and the ANC in general were thereafter condemned as "terrorists." Then, in 1985, Tambo rejected on Mandela's behalf Prime Minister **Pieter Willem Botha**'s offer of release from prison if

Nelson Mandela in the Mandela and Tambo Law Office, 1952. *Courtesy of Jurgen Schadeberg.*

he would reject violence and end the armed struggle as a prelude to negotiations. Tambo's rejection was then affirmed by **Zindzi Mandela** when she read out at Jabulani Stadium in **Soweto** Mandela's own words from a speech he had prepared. Following P. W. Botha's government "reforms" that further exacerbated the effects of apartheid, Tambo approved the call to make the country "ungovernable," unleashing the radical and often violent rolling mass action of township youth. Tambo, nevertheless, remained committed to diplomacy and hopes for a democratic country. Following the official unbanning of the ANC in 1990, Tambo returned to South Africa from his nearly thirty years in exile. Despite the pressures of his work and significant health challenges, including repeated and increasingly intense strokes, he continued to serve the ANC, latterly in the honorific role as national chairman when Mandela was elected as president of the party. In 1991, he was instrumental in the formulation of the Commonwealth's Harare Declaration which reaffirmed self-determination, equality, and global peace. He died in April of 1993 of complications from a massive stroke just about a year before the first all-democratic elections.

THEMBU PEOPLE AND REGION. Nelson Mandela's upbringing and ethnic origins are associated with the Thembu group. The Thembu were established in the coastal region of the Eastern Cape from at least the early sixteenth century or earlier and were part of the wider Nguni-speaking peoples of southern Africa who spoke the Xhosa dialect. Nguni-speakers were in turn part of the much larger Bantu languages family that had its origin among peoples who migrated in a series of movements from West Africa from about 1000 BCE, with a major stream arriving in the eastern coastal areas of South Africa around 300 CE. Other polities in the area include the Bhaca, Bomvana, Mfengu, Mpondo, Mpondomise, and Xesibe. The Thembu were, as with other Nguni-speaking societies, primarily agro-pastoralists who also engaged in some regional trade, and families were usually headed by a patriarchal male, though some female-headed households did exist. Beyond the family, elders educated the youth, who came of age in gendered cohorts through separate male and female initiation ceremonies. Males, including Mandela himself, traditionally also underwent "*ulwaluko,*" or circumcision, as part of the process of entering "manhood." The Thembu settled in the Mbashe River valley area in the heart of the present-day Transkei (see map) around 1600 CE and took advantage of the well rain- and river-watered coastal areas to develop a robust political economy with mixed farming, cattle, and to a lesser extent sheep, with herding as well as complex hierarchal leadership structures based around the office of chief under the authority of a paramount or king. Among the Nguni-speakers, chiefs were understood to govern by consensus and through democratic forms of consultation and consensus-seeking with leading men. Prior to the advent of White conquest and settlement beginning in the eighteenth century, segmentation among leading households was common as young men who did not stand to inherit the chieftainship split off to establish separate chiefdoms in the region where open land was then relatively abundant. This practice was governed by the Nguni-speakers rules of inheritance for polygynous families where chiefly husbands designated a senior "right hand" wife whose first male issue succeeded the father and a lesser or "left hand" wife whose issue did not inherit.

Thembu chiefs paid a limited allegiance to a founding paramount dynasty and remained open over time to incorporating people from other ethnic groups in the region. Nkosi (great chief) Vusani Ngubencuka, who was Mandela's patrilineal great grandfather, consolidated the Thembu under the Hala royal clan before his death in 1830. This was no easy feat. Beginning in the 1820s, in a context of increasing competition for cattle, the central productive and reproductive economic resource, people, probably fleeing drought and famine in the interior (associated with the much-debated historical concept known as the Mfecane) as well as neighboring Sotho and Bhaca, raided the Thembu and threatened the integrity of the chiefdom. By the 1830s, White settlers from Cape Town and environs posed an even greater challenge to Africans, including the Xhosa and the Thembu in the Eastern Cape area, as they penetrated, conquered, and transformed the region. These Whites, predominantly disaffected Afrikaners (people primarily descended from the Dutch who settled the Cape following the arrival of the Dutch East India Company, VOC, in 1652), as well as a range of Christian missionary societies and British merchants, brought both pressure and new opportunities to the Transkei. While the primarily pastoralist Afrikaners, who rejected the newly established British domination of the Cape, clashed with Africans over control of grazing lands in the Transkei, beyond the formal British Cape Colony, missionaries sought to convert and coopt the people. The British Cape colonial government then extended its power into the area, in part as an effort to stabilize the region as a labor pool. The Thembu agreed to a rapprochement of sorts with the British, accepting some degree of protection against the persistent threats of cattle raids and tensions among African societies, which had been exacerbated by attacks by refugees from the interior as well as settler incursions. One section of the Thembu relocated into what was then part of the British Cape Colony, only later to be pressured to move and settle in the designated Emigrant Thembuland. Meanwhile, succession disputes among rivals for the paramountcy yielded the rise of chief Ngangelizwe

who, despite provoking an ill-advised war with the neighboring Gcaleka Xhosa under chief Sarhili, managed to retain the bulk of original Thembu lands in the Transkei. In an ill-fated gambit, the Thembu then decided to throw their lot in with the British colonial government in hopes of gaining some degree of security for their land and people. As pressures mounted, Thembu leaders bargained for colonial safeguards from competing Africans at the cost of protections for their independence. Following a devastating cattle epidemic and ensuing famine, referred to as the Xhosa Cattle Killing, in the 1830s, the Thembu entered into protracted negotiations with the Cape government to have their territory incorporated into the colony. Despite British Imperial vacillations, the then self-governing Cape Colony began an annexation process for the Thembuland Territory in 1876, though it was not completed until 1885. The process established the four magistracies of Xalanga, St. Marks, Elliot, and Engcobo that the Thembu had called for, and some legal provisions to maintain traditional chiefly authority. It also extended the very limited Cape franchise for qualified Africans to some Thembu, though this would be short-lived, and ostensibly protected the land for African occupation. Notwithstanding some significant efforts at rebellion against the colony among a number of disaffected people in the early 1880s, many Thembu had by then acculturated to the colonial economy and especially Christianity, though a decidedly separatist independent Thembu Church emerged at the same time. These divisions within Thembu society deepened in the ensuring years and account for some views suggesting that the Thembu, and by extension even Mandela himself, exhibited collaborationist tendencies that may have later emerged in the negotiated settlement to end White rule in the 1990s. Thembuland was ultimately fully incorporated into a segregated Transkeian Territories as part of the later apartheid-era Bantustan system and is currently a part of Eastern Cape Province.

TREASON TRIAL (March 19, 1956–March 29, 1961). As part of its efforts to quell opposition to the full articulation of its apartheid policies, the South African state lashed out at a wide range of political leaders, including Nelson Mandela, through the application of its sweeping Suppression of Communism Act. Following growing **African National Congress** (ANC) mass action and the **Congress of the People**'s declaration of the **Freedom Charter** (see appendix A), from later 1955 through March of 1956, South African police raided dozens of homes and offices across the country, arresting more than 156 people, and charged them with high treason for their work in or association with activities deemed to be "communist" and so intended to bring about the end of the state. Among those charged, alongside Mandela, were prominent members of the **Congress of Democrats** (COD), the ANC, the South African Communist Party (SACP), and the South African Indian Congress (SAIC). They included **Chief Albert Luthuli**, president of the ANC, **Oliver Tambo**, **Walter Sisulu**, **Yusuf Dadoo**, **Ahmed Kathrada**, **Lionel "Rusty" Bernstein**, Ruth First, **and Joe Slovo**, who also served with **Bram Fischer** and Mandela as counsel for the defense. Although the charges and potential outcomes were grave, the proceedings

Nelson Mandela outside Treason Trial, 1952. *Courtesy of Jurgen Schadeberg.*

Nelson Mandela (center) with L–Dr. James Moroka, President of the ANC and R–Yusuf Dadoo, Chairman of the South African Communist Party and South African Indian Congress, 1952 Treason Trial. *Courtesy of Jurgen Schadeberg.*

turned into something of a show trial for both the state and the defendants. The case for the prosecution appeared, from the start, to be tenuous and there was a considerable sense of excitement among the defendants and their many thousands of supporters who felt the trial would show clearly how misguided the government and its policies were. Many sang *Nkosi Sikeleli y Afrika* (God Bless Africa), the ANC and later South African national anthem, and Mandela provided moving testimony outlining the ANC's vision for democracy in the country. The state prosecution's case, however, quickly collapsed for procedural reasons as well as lack of contingent evidence, and all but thirty defendants were released. Mandela was among the remaining defendants for whom the state claimed more compelling evidence. In the end, he and the others were released based on the judge's findings that the state had failed to show that the ANC was a "communist" organization. The trial, nevertheless, brought Mandela to the attention of the state security forces and the world not long before he would be imprisoned for life on Robben Island and it demonstrated that, to a large extent, South African still had an independent, fair minded judiciary.

TSHUKUDU, ADELAIDE FRANCES. See TAMBO, ADELAIDE FRANCES

TUTU, DESMOND MPILO (October 7, 1931–). The Anglican Archbishop of Cape Town from 1986–1996, Desmond Tutu was an antiapartheid and human rights activist whom Nelson Mandela appointed to serve as the chair of the South African Truth and Reconciliation Commission (TRC). After an early career as a teacher, Tutu joined the clergy and used his position as a Christian leader of various congregations, and as the Secretary General of the Council of South African Churches from 1978–

1985 as a bully pulpit to oppose apartheid. He appeared at antiapartheid events on a number of occasions with **Winnie Madikizela-Mandela** as she rose to prominence as the proxy voice of Nelson Mandela, and he supported the campaign for international sanctions against South Africa in the 1980s. In 1985, he was awarded the Nobel Peace Prize, an honor shared with just three other South Africans including **Chief Albert Luthuli, F. W. de Klerk,** and Mandela. Although Mandela had great confidence in Tutu's leadership, especially of the TRC, the two clashed, often publicly, during much of Mandela's time as president. Tutu openly criticized Mandela and ANC leaders for what he claimed were self-indulgent tendencies, even to the extent of condemning Mandela's signature colorful shirts as too flamboyant and expensive. They remained, however, respectful colleagues through the end of Mandela's presidency.

U

UMKHONTO WE SIZWE (MK, the Spear of the Nation). Umkhonto We Sizwe (MK), the brainchild of Nelson Mandela, **Joe Slovo**, and others, was the underground military wing of the **African National Congress** (ANC). It had its origins in the aftermath of the apartheid government's horrific attack by police on unarmed protestors during the Sharpeville Massacre in 1960. Mandela and others who had hitherto remained committed to peaceful tactics of mass passive resistance that included marches, rallies, passbook (the hated documents that Blacks were compelled by law to carry when living and working in South Africa's "Whites-only" areas that constituted the vast majority of the country), burnings, protests, and defiance of what they saw as unjust laws. At every turn, their efforts were rebuffed and met with a range of repressive tactics including police harassment, banning (a legal sanction that prevented a person or organization from operating or associating with others freely), and arrests with up to ninety-day detentions. As the stakes escalated, Mandela became convinced that since the oppressor dictated the terms of the conflict, the ANC would have no choice but to abandon nonviolence and engage in an armed struggle. He first laid out his M-Plan, a structure modeled on other revolutionary movements such as in Cuba, which arranged for secret cells to operate underground and limit the risk of discovery by state security police. The ANC leadership forged ahead with setting up the foundations of MK at what was to be the secret base of Liliesleaf Farm in Rivonia. Prior to that location being compromised, Mandela, **Walter Sisulu**, **Denis Goldberg, Rusty Bernstein, Govan Mbeki**, and others met there to plan Operation Mayibuye, which aimed to infiltrate the country with trained operatives and to conduct sabotage to destabilize and so compel the apartheid government to accept a democratic solution. In order to facilitate MK operations, the ANC sent Mandela out of the country in early 1962 on a **tour of Africa** in order to gain support for the ANC as well as to get training in the military tactics and strategies for insurgency. Prior to his departure, in June of 1960, Mandela notified the South African press of MK's existence and plans to engage in a campaign of sabotage, leading MK to be labeled as a terrorist organization. Then, on December 16, 1960, MK began a bombing campaign against government buildings and infrastructure. After a few successes in bombing government electricity pylons and buildings, MK struggled to make inroads. Few members were properly trained in the use of explosives and state security forces easily penetrated many of the underground cells. It was not until into the later 1970s, after the **Soweto** uprising of 1975 where South African Black youth engaged in mass defiance against apartheid education policies, that a surge of new recruits led to a more robust capacity for MK. By the early 1980s, under the leadership of both Slovo and the new chief of MK, Ronnie Kasrils, a White communist and member of the ANC who had received military training in the Soviet Union, MK was operationally more successful than previously. These successes, however, came with at a cost. A number of bombings, especially at Magoo's bar, a nightspot on the

Durban beachfront that was popular with young White liberals, included otherwise sympathetic White civilians. This added to growing fears of the ANC as a terrorist organization, and perceptions of Mandela as the driver of violent insurrection. The Truth and Reconciliation Commission (TRC) of South Africa found MK to have perpetrated human-rights violations for this bombing, and for the use of torture in its training camps outside the country. Mandela largely dismissed these accusations, arguing that there was not a moral equivalency with the apartheid state's use of violence. MK was disbanded and melded into the new South African Defence Force after 1990 as part of the negotiated settlement for a democratic South Africa.

UNIVERSITY OF FORT HARE. Founded in 1916 in Alice, Eastern Cape, by the Wesleyan Missionary Society, this was the first and premier institution of higher education for Blacks in South Africa until the end of the apartheid era. Built on the site of the early settler Fort Hare that was established during British colonial wars of expansion against the **Thembu-Xhosa**, the university college played a critical role as the higher education home of many antiapartheid leaders such as, **Govan Mbeki**, Robert Sobukwe, and **Oliver Tambo**, as well as future Bantustan leaders such as **Chief Mangosuthu Buthelezi** of the Inkatha Freedom Party (IFP) and **Kaiser Matanzima** of the Transkei. It also hosted a number of prominent anticolonial leaders from across Africa such as Kenneth Kaunda, Sir Seretse Khama, Julius Nyerere, Robert Mugabe, and Joshua Nkomo,

and also served as an incubator of resistance ideologies. Originally known as the South African Native College and associated with the University of South Africa, it later developed an association with Rhodes University. Among its leading African academic staff were the celebrated Davidson Don Tengo Jabavu and Professor Zachariah Keodirelang Matthews. In keeping with **Chief Jongitaba Dalindyebo**'s plan for him to become an advisor, and his own interests in law, Nelson Mandela enrolled at the college in 1939 and studied English, anthropology, politics, native administration, and Roman Dutch law. He also became involved in drama club, ballroom dancing, and teaching Bible classes for the Student Christian Association. Although he kept his distance from student members of the **African National Congress** (ANC), it was at Fort Hare that Mandela got his first taste of political activism when he was elected to the student representative council. When students, including his new friend and mentor Tambo, who was president of the Student Representative Council at the time, boycotted the elections as part of a broader protest over the quality of food provided at the college, Mandela decided to resign from the council because of the underrepresentative poll. The stern college principal, Alexander Kerr, warned Mandela that he would be expelled if he did no fulfill his responsibilities as an elected student councilor. Mandela refused to bow to Kerr's directive and, despite admonitions from an angry Chief Dalindyebo, Mandela left the college without completing his studies there.

WILLIAMS, CECIL (1906–1979). Cecil Williams, communist and antiapartheid activist, is best known for being arrested with Mandela in 1962 as they traveled around South Africa. Mandela posed as **David Motsamayi**, Williams' African chauffer, in a ruse to move about while Mandela was wanted by police during his Black Pimpernel period prior to his long incarceration. The UK-born Williams moved to South Africa in 1928, working first as a schoolteacher and then in theater as a writer-producer-director and actor. Williams was an active leader in the Springbok League, an antiapartheid organization supported primarily by White liberals and radicals, including **Bram Fischer**, and in the **Congress of Democrats** (COD) where he worked with Ruth First and **Rusty Bernstein**. Williams was banned by the state for his membership in the South African Communist Party (SACP) and he later joined **Umkhonto We Sizwe (MK)**, where he first met Mandela. Often assaulted for being gay, Williams was a tireless advocate of nonracialism and his work with Mandela has been chronicled in the film *The Man Who Drove Mandela* (1998, Jezebel Productions). Donald Rickard, U.S. Vice-Consul in Durban and then working for the American Central Intelligence Agency, by his own admission, alleges he provided the tipoff that led to Williams' arrest with Mandela on August 5, 1962, while the two were driving to **Johannesburg** in an Austin Westminster automobile, just outside Howick, KwaZulu-Natal. A statue now commemorates the arrest at the Mandela Capture Site. Mandela had just conducted several secret meetings with **Chief** Albert Luthuli, then-president of the ANC and other leading ANC and MK officials. Williams was released not long after his arrest, and returned to the United Kingdom, where he died in 1979.

WOMEN, NELSON MANDELA AND. Throughout his life, Nelson Mandela championed women's causes and equal rights in public, although he sometimes had an ambiguous personal relationship with them. First and foremost, Mandela advocated for women to play a leading role in the struggle. He worked closely with a number of important women and supported them in the **African National Congress** (ANC), the South African Indian Congress (SAIC), and the South African Communist Party (SACP). From the 1940s, he valued the counsel and leadership of **Albertina Sisulu**, the wife of his friend and patron **Walter Sisulu**, as she helped forge the ANC Women's League. Ruth First, wife of **Joe Slovo**, the cofounder with Mandela of **Umkhonto We Sizwe (MK)**, was also a close friend and collaborator. He also spoke publicly of the need to have women in mainstream leadership roles, and so he supported Lilian Ngoyi's election to the ANC Executive Committee in 1956. His marriage to **Evelyn Mase** was, however, fraught with challenges as he devoted himself ever more to politics and the struggle. That may have accounted, but not excused, his distancing himself from her and the children as he sought out **Winnie Madikizela-Mandela**, and the more troubling accusations of spousal assault for allegedly grabbing and shaking Evelyn in a moment of

Nelson Mandela and Ruth First, wife of Joe Slovo, 1952. *Courtesy of Jurgen Schadeberg.*

skilled words of later Nobel Laureate **Nadine Gordimer**, who was a devoted fan and helped him draft his famous "I am prepared to die" speech from the dock during the **Rivonia Trial**, a treatise that may have helped him avoid the death penalty. Still, his loyalty to Winnie was perhaps too blinded by love, and he found it difficult to see her excesses and corruption for what it was. Following the painful and politicized divorce, he found a good match with the wife of a fellow liberation leader, **Graça Machel**. Mandela himself often quipped about how much he enjoyed his amorous relations with women, yet he was at the forefront of working to ensure their rights in the new South Africa. He hand a strong hand in shaping the specific rights to women that were enshrined in the new constitution in 1996. Indeed, the document is one of the few in the world that guarantees specific allocations of representation for women in parliament. Additionally, he affirmed South Africa's adoption of the United Nations Convention for the Prevention of Discrimination Against Women. Overall, his public and political support for women's rights and for women in leadership transformed the South African political landscape.

anger. He certainly promoted Winnie's rise to political fame, despite, or possibly because of, the limits of his imprisonment from 1963 to 1990. Two of the most prominent biographers of Mandela were women who worked closely with and admired him, **Mary Benson** and **Fatima Meer**. He even entrusted his life to the

X

XHOSA. See THEMBU PEOPLE AND REGION

Z

ZUMA, JACOB GEDLEYIHLEKISA (April 12, 1942–). A controversial figure who served as president of South Africa from 2009 to 2018 when he was compelled to resign over charges of corruption, Jacob Zuma is a long-serving **African National Congress** (ANC) party stalwart who has been discredited for corrupt and criminal behaviors. Zuma came from a humble background. Raised in the Nkandhla district in the heart of the old Zulu kingdom in KwaZulu-Natal, Zuma's mother was a domestic worker and his father, who passed when his son was just five, was a local constable. Zuma was not educated in formal Western schools but learned to read and write on his own initiative as well as learning about the customs and culture of resistance in Zulu society while working as a cattle herd boy in his youth. It was these experiences that informed his populist political image as a man of the people. In 1959 at the age of seventeen, influenced by the trade union movement in Durban, Zuma joined the ANC Youth League and the South African Union of Trade Unions, an organization allied with the ANC. Not long after it was founded, he joined **Umkhonto We Sizwe (MK)**, the armed wing of the ANC, and got involved in clandestine operations associated with the armed struggle. State security forces arrested Zuma in 1963 as he and forty-five other members of MK attempted to leave South Africa for Zambia to undertake military training. Following being tortured in jail, Zuma was tried, convicted, and sentenced to ten years in prison. Zuma served his sentence on Robben Island, though he did not have contact with Nelson Mandela during that time. On his release, he resumed his work with MK. After numerous brushes with South African state security, he went into exile in Swaziland, where he worked closely with **Thabo Mbeki**, Mandela's successor as president, and then to Mozambique. Following the unbanning of the ANC and the first elections, Zuma returned to serve in Mandela's government. His political fortunes rose while simultaneously he became further mired in corruption and controversy. In 1997, he was elected deputy president of the ANC, and this led, in 1999, to his appointment as deputy president under Mbeki's presidency. Mbeki, however, dismissed Zuma from this post over a number of allegations of dubious activities while in exile as well as corruption and graft. Zuma remained mired in scandal for fraud and a rape charge, all for which he narrowly escaped convictions. After his dismissal his fortunes fell for a time. Yet in a bid that some saw as a misguided effort to save the ANC from scandal, reports suggest that Mandela, who often expressed his fondness for Zuma, stepped in on a number of occasions to bail Zuma out of debt and steer him away from relations with corrupt figures. In part because of Mandela's financial assistance, Zuma rebounded and rose to prominence in the party. He was able to ride a groundswell of disaffection with Mbeki's presidency, forcing Mbeki's resignation in 2008 and leading to the custodial eight-month interim presidency of Kgalema Motlanthe. In what some saw as a major shift in party politics, Zuma was elected president of the ANC in 2009 and by extension to the presidency as leader of the majority party. He served as president until 2018, although he was mired in continuous scandals and faced repeated criminal charges for fraud and corruption, including for his financing with state funds massive renovations to his personal home in Nkandhla, and for associations with the notorious Schaik Shabir, his financial advisor. Zuma's actions were later described as part of the infamous "state capture" in investigations over corrupt private interests controlling the South African government. Zuma was finally forced from the presidency in 2018 and was succeeded by **Cyril Ramaphosa**, whom some believe was the heir apparent that Mandela would have preferred over Mbeki to replace him.

Appendix A

Freedom Charter

This became the guiding document for the goals of the African National Congress and later was the foundation for the South African Constitution in 1996.

As adopted at the Congress of the People, Kliptown, South Africa, June 26, 1955.

We, the People of South Africa, declare for all our country and the world to know:

that South Africa belongs to all who live in it, black and white, and that no government can justly claim authority unless it is based on the will of all the people;

that our people have been robbed of their birthright to land, liberty and peace by a form of government founded on injustice and inequality;

that our country will never be prosperous or free until all our people live in brotherhood, enjoying equal rights and opportunities;

that only a democratic state, based on the will of all the people, can secure to all their birthright without distinction of color, race, sex or belief;

And therefore, we, the people of South Africa, black and white together equals, countrymen and brothers adopt this Freedom Charter;

And we pledge ourselves to strive together, sparing neither strength nor courage, until the democratic changes here set out have been won.

The People Shall Govern!

Every man and woman shall have the right to vote for and to stand as a candidate for all bodies which make laws;

All people shall be entitled to take part in the administration of the country;

The rights of the people shall be the same, regardless of race, color or sex;

All bodies of minority rule, advisory boards, councils and authorities shall be replaced by democratic organs of self-government.

All National Groups Shall have Equal Rights!

There shall be equal status in the bodies of state, in the courts and in the schools for all national groups and races;

All people shall have equal right to use their own languages, and to develop their own folk culture and customs;

All national groups shall be protected by law against insults to their race and national pride;

The preaching and practice of national, race or color discrimination and contempt shall be a punishable crime;

All apartheid laws and practices shall be set aside.

The People Shall Share in the Country's Wealth!

The national wealth of our country, the heritage of South Africans, shall be restored to the people;

The mineral wealth beneath the soil, the Banks and monopoly industry shall be transferred to the ownership of the people as a whole;

All other industry and trade shall be controlled to assist the wellbeing of the people;

All people shall have equal rights to trade where they choose, to manufacture and to enter all trades, crafts and professions.

The Land Shall be Shared Among Those Who Work It!

Restrictions of land ownership on a racial basis shall be ended, and all the land re-divided amongst those who work it to banish famine and land hunger;

The state shall help the peasants with implements, seed, tractors and dams to save the soil and assist the tillers;

Freedom of movement shall be guaranteed to all who work on the land;

All shall have the right to occupy land wherever they choose;

People shall not be robbed of their cattle, and forced labor and farm prisons shall be abolished.

All Shall be Equal Before the Law!

No-one shall be imprisoned, deported or restricted without a fair trial; No-one shall be condemned by the order of any Government official;

The courts shall be representative of all the people;

Imprisonment shall be only for serious crimes against the people, and shall aim at re-education, not vengeance;

The police force and army shall be open to all on an equal basis and shall be the helpers and protectors of the people;

All laws which discriminate on grounds of race, color or belief shall be repealed.

All Shall Enjoy Equal Human Rights!

The law shall guarantee to all their right to speak, to organize, to meet together, to publish, to preach, to worship and to educate their children;

The privacy of the house from police raids shall be protected by law;

All shall be free to travel without restriction from countryside to town, from province to province, and from South Africa abroad;

Pass Laws, permits and all other laws restricting these freedoms shall be abolished.

There Shall be Work and Security!

All who work shall be free to form trade unions, to elect their officers and to make wage agreements with their employers;

The state shall recognize the right and duty of all to work, and to draw full unemployment benefits;

Men and women of all races shall receive equal pay for equal work;

There shall be a forty-hour working week, a national minimum wage, paid annual leave, and sick leave for all workers, and maternity leave on full pay for all working mothers;

Miners, domestic workers, farm workers and civil servants shall have the same rights as all others who work;

Child labor, compound labor, the tot system and contract labor shall be abolished.

The Doors of Learning and Culture Shall be Opened!

The government shall discover, develop and encourage national talent for the enhancement of our cultural life;

All the cultural treasures of mankind shall be open to all, by free exchange of books, ideas and contact with other lands;

The aim of education shall be to teach the youth to love their people and their culture, to honor human brotherhood, liberty and peace;

Education shall be free, compulsory, universal and equal for all children; Higher education and technical training shall be opened to all by means of state allowances and scholarships awarded on the basis of merit;

Adult illiteracy shall be ended by a mass state education plan;

Teachers shall have all the rights of other citizens;

The color bar in cultural life, in sport and in education shall be abolished.

There Shall be Houses, Security and Comfort!

All people shall have the right to live where they choose, be decently housed, and to bring up their families in comfort and security;

Unused housing space to be made available to the people;

Rent and prices shall be lowered, food plentiful and no-one shall go hungry;

A preventive health scheme shall be run by the state;

Free medical care and hospitalization shall be provided for all, with special care for mothers and young children;

Slums shall be demolished, and new suburbs built where all have transport, roads, lighting, playing fields, creches and social centers;

The aged, the orphans, the disabled and the sick shall be cared for by the state;

Rest, leisure and recreation shall be the right of all:

Fenced locations and ghettoes shall be abolished, and laws which break up families shall be repealed.

There Shall be Peace and Friendship!

South Africa shall be a fully independent state which respects the rights and sovereignty of all nations;

South Africa shall strive to maintain world peace and the settlement of all international disputes by negotiation—not war;

Peace and friendship amongst all our people shall be secured by upholding the equal rights, opportunities and status of all;

The people of the protectorates Basutoland, Bechuanaland and Swaziland shall be free to decide for themselves their own future;

The right of all peoples of Africa to independence and self-government shall be recognized, and shall be the basis of close co-operation.

Let all people who love their people and their country now say, as we say here:

THESE FREEDOMS WE WILL FIGHT FOR, SIDE BY SIDE, THROUGHOUT OUR LIVES, UNTIL WE HAVE WON OUR LIBERTY.

Source: African National Congress. https://www.anc1912.org.za/.

Appendix B

Mandela's Speeches

NELSON MANDELA'S SPEECH FROM THE DOCK, 1962 TRIAL FOR INCITEMENT

Place: Old Synagogue Court Pretoria South Africa, November 7, 1962

Presentation notes: At the end of this trial, Mandela was convicted and sentenced to three years' imprisonment on the charge of incitement and two years for leaving the country without valid travel documents.

I am charged with inciting people to commit an offence by way of protest against the law, a law which neither I nor any of my people had any say in preparing. The law against which the protest was directed is the law which established a republic in the Union of South Africa. I am also charged with leaving the country without a passport. This court has found that I am guilty of incitement to commit an offence in opposition to this law as well as of leaving the country. But in weighing up the decision as to the sentence which is to be imposed for such an offence, the court must take into account the question of responsibility, whether it is I who is responsible or whether, in fact, a large measure of the responsibility does not lie on the shoulders of the government which promulgated that law, knowing that my people, who constitute the majority of the population of this country, were opposed to that law, and knowing further that every legal means of demonstrating that opposition had been closed to them by prior legislation, and by government administrative action . . .

Many years ago, when I was a boy brought up in my village in the Transkei, I listened to the elders of the tribe telling stories about the good old days, before the arrival of the white man. Then our people lived peacefully, under the democratic rule of their kings and their *amapakati,* and moved freely and confidently up and down the country without let or hindrance. Then the country was ours, in our own name and right. We occupied the land, the forests, the rivers; we extracted the mineral wealth beneath the soil and all the riches of this beautiful country. We set up and operated our own government, we controlled our own armies and we organized our own trade and commerce. The elders would tell tales of the wars fought by our ancestors in defense of the fatherland, as well as the acts of valor performed by generals and soldiers during those epic days. The names of Dingane and Bambata, among the Zulus, of Hintsa, Makana, Ndlambe of the AmaXhosa, of Sekhukhuni and others in the north, were mentioned as the pride and glory of the entire African nation . . .

The starting point in the case against me is the holding of the conference in Pietermaritzburg on 25 and 26 March last year [1961], known as the All-in

African Conference, which was called by a committee which had been established by leading people and spokesmen of the whole African population, to consider the situation which was being created by the promulgation of the republic in the country, without consultation with us, and without our consent. That conference unanimously rejected the decision of the government, acting only in the name of and with the agreement of the white minority of this country, to establish a republic.

Government violence can do only one thing, and that is to breed counter violence. We have warned repeatedly that the government, by resorting continually to violence, will breed in this country counter-violence amongst the people, till ultimately, if there is no dawning of sanity on the part of the government—ultimately, the dispute between the government and my people will finish up by being settled in violence and by force. Already there are indications in this country that people, my people, Africans, are turning to deliberate acts of violence and of force against the government, in order to persuade the government, in the only language which this government shows by its own behavior that it understands.

Source: Nelson Mandela Foundation. https://www.nelsonmandela.org/.

NELSON MANDELA "I AM PREPARED TO DIE" SPEECH AT THE RIVONIA TRIAL

Statement from the dock at the opening of the defense case in the Rivonia Trial, Palace of Justice, Pretoria Supreme Court Pretoria South Africa, April 20, 1964.

NOTES: Nelson Mandela together with Walter Sisulu, Govan Mbeki, Raymond Mhlaba, Elias Motsoaledi, Andrew Mlangeni, Ahmed Kathrada, and Denis Goldberg were convicted on June 11, 1964, of planning to overthrow the South African government by means of violence and for acts of sabotage, and were sentenced to life imprisonment. Mandela was already in jail at the time, serving five years for political agitation and for having left the country on his tour of Africa without lawful permission. Mandela departed from his prepared speech. Both the verbatim and prepared speeches are reproduced. The court proceedings at the Rivonia Trial were recorded by the State on dictabelt for which there is now no playback equipment. Mandela's statement from the dock was digitized with the assistance of the British Library, and this digital recording is now in the custody of the National Archives of South Africa. This recording was used to transcribe this speech—the verbatim transcript. The speech is approximately 176 minutes long.

Explanations: The first seven were to spend most of their incarceration on Robben Island. Denis Goldberg, as a white male, spent his incarceration at Pretoria Maximum Prison because apartheid policies applied to prisons as well. Robben Island was reserved for African, Coloured, and Indian prisoners. Arthur Goldreich was among those arrested in connection with the Rivonia Trial. On August 11, 1963, he together with Harold Wolpe, Abdulhay Jassat, and Moosa "Mosie" Moolla escaped from jail by bribing a guard, and fled the country. Liliesleaf was the name of the farm in the district of Rivonia on the northern outskirts of Johannesburg. It was owned by the South African Communist Party, and Goldreich and his family lived in the main house as the "white owners."

My Lord, I am the First Accused.

I hold a Bachelor's Degree in Arts and practiced as an attorney in Johannesburg for a number of years in partnership with Mr. Oliver Tambo, a co-conspirator in this case. I am a convicted prisoner serving five years for leaving the country without a permit and for inciting people to go on strike at the end of May 1961.

I admit immediately that I was one of the persons who helped to form Umkhonto we Sizwe, and that I played a prominent role in its affairs until I was arrested in August 1962. In the statement which I am about to make, I shall correct certain false impressions which have been created by State witnesses; amongst other things I will demonstrate that certain of the acts referred to in the evidence were not, and could not have been committed by Umkhonto. I will also deal with the relationship between the African National Congress and with the part which I personally have played in the affairs of both organizations. I shall deal also with the part played by the Communist Party. In order to explain these matters properly, I will have to explain what Umkhonto set out to achieve; what methods it prescribed for the achievement of these objects, and why these methods were chosen. I will also have to explain how I became involved in the activities of these organizations.

At the outset, I want to say that the suggestion made by the state in its opening that the struggle in South Africa is under the influence of foreigners or communists is wholly incorrect. I have done whatever I did, both as an individual and as a leader of my people, because of my experience in South Africa and my own proudly felt African background, and not because of what any outsider might have said.

In my youth in the Transkei I listened to the elders of my tribe telling stories of the old days. Amongst the tales they related to me were those of wars fought by our ancestors in defence of the fatherland. The names of Dingane and Bambatha, Hintsa and Makana, Squngathi and Dalasile, Moshoeshoe and Sekhukhune were praised as the pride and the glory of the entire African nation. I hoped then that life might offer me the opportunity to serve my people and make my own humble contribution to their freedom struggle. This is what has motivated me in all that I have done in relation to the charges made against me in this case. . . .

Having said this, I must deal immediately and at some length with the question of sabotage. Some of the things so far told to the Court are true and some are untrue. I do not however, deny that I planned sabotage. I did not plan it in a spirit of recklessness, nor because I have any love for violence. I planned it as a result of a calm and sober assessment of the political situation that had arisen after many years of tyranny, exploitation, and oppression of my people by the whites. . . .

The African National Congress was formed in 1912 to defend the rights of the African people which had been seriously curtailed by the South Africa Act, and which were then being threatened by the Native Land Act. For thirty-seven years—that is until 1949— it adhered strictly to a constitutional struggle. It put forward demands and resolutions; it sent delegations to the Government in the belief that African grievances could be settled through peaceful discussion and that Africans could advance gradually to full political rights. But white governments remained unmoved, and the rights of Africans became less instead of becoming greater . . .

Africans want to be paid a living wage. Africans want to perform work which they are capable of doing, and not work which the Government declares them to be capable of. Africans want to be allowed to live where they obtain work, and not be endorsed out of an area because they were not born there. Africans want to be allowed to own land in places where they work, and not to be obliged to live in rented houses which they can never call their own. Africans want to be part of the general population, and not confined to living in their own ghettoes. African men want to have their wives and children to live with them where they work, and not be forced into an unnatural existence in men's hostels. African women want to be with their menfolk and not be left permanently widowed in the Reserves. Africans want to be allowed out after eleven o'clock at night and not to be confined to their rooms like little children. Africans want to be allowed to travel in their own country and to seek work where they want to and not where the Labour Bureau tells them to. Africans want a just share in the whole of South Africa; they want security and a stake in society.

Above all, we want equal political rights, because without them our disabilities will be permanent. I know this sounds revolutionary to the whites in this country, because the majority of voters will be Africans. This makes the white man fear democracy.

But this fear cannot be allowed to stand in the way of the only solution which will guarantee racial harmony and freedom for all. It is not true that the enfranchisement of all will result in racial domination. Political division, based on color, is entirely artificial and, when it disappears, so will the domination of one color group by another. The ANC has spent half a century fighting against racialism. When it triumphs it will not change that policy.

This then is what the ANC is fighting. Their struggle is a truly national one. It is a struggle of the African people, inspired by their own suffering and their own experience. It is a struggle for the right to live.

During my lifetime I have dedicated myself to this struggle of the African people. I have fought against white domination, and I have fought against black domination. I have cherished the ideal of a democratic and free society in which all persons live together in harmony and with equal opportunities. It is an ideal which I hope to live for and to achieve. But if needs be, it is an ideal for which I am prepared to die.

Source: Nelson Mandela Foundation. https://www.nelsonmandela.org/.

Bibliography

CONTENTS

Writing related to Nelson Mandela's life and work reflects an abiding concern with the struggle against racism, oppression, and exploitation both in South Africa and around the world, and it falls into three broad categories: scholarly academic works, principally in the fields of history, politics, and political economy; works of political advocacy and propaganda, of which few are listed in this bibliography due to the limited and often ephemeral nature of their publication; and popular works that celebrate, though sometimes exploit, the iconic image of Mandela. While the general scholarly works probably outnumber popular works, the use of the Mandela image and persona as a sort of global brand took on a life of their own, and grew exponentially in the period between his release from prison in 1990, through his term as president in 1994, and until just after his passing in 2013.

The bibliography reflects primarily scholarly works related to Nelson Mandela and South Africa that were part of broader studies about anti-imperialism and African nationalism. These analyses of the political economy of South Africa and studies of the African National Congress as a revolutionary national liberation movement were informed by the earlier Russian revolution and the spread of trade unionism and international socialism. Moreover, they emerged in a context where the new schools of Left or Radical History and political economy were taking root in the academy. Writing about African societies and history also built upon earlier works by missionaries and subsequent scholarship in the fields of anthropology and ethnography. Indeed, an appreciation of the converging strands of left history and anthropology is essential to a general understanding of African studies as well as Mandela's place in it. While many radical scholars emphasized the class dimensions of the struggle in the context of industrial capitalism and the migrant labor environment of South Africa, others focused on the African nationalist dimensions of his and the ANC's work where race and class intersected. Anyone interested in a full understanding of Nelson Mandela and the context he worked and lived in would be best served by a close reading of the listed works in African anthropology, history, political science, and general African studies. Mandela, as with African nationalism, was after all a synthesis of indigenous cultures, history, and identity with Western education and experiences.

Mandela's work and identity are almost synonymous with that of the African National Congress from the time of his joining it in 1943. In this regard, histories of the ANC and the wider opposition movement to apartheid are an essential dimension to understanding his life and politics. Mandela emerged as a political leader in a historical moment when he and his youthful colleagues were able to challenge the old guard of the party. Understanding the background to African politics in general and the ANC in particular is only possible through the works that trace the development of Black politics from the earliest periods of primary resistance to imperial intrusion and colonial rule through the political consciousness that emerged with transformation of Africans into wage workers. Thus, works on the early and later history of the ANC show the unique relationship between African "traditionalism," Black Consciousness, and the ideals of African socialism.

The political and legal environment in which many of the works on history and political economy were often crafted and published was fraught with complications and challenges, to say the least. Many of the scholars and political leaders who wrote these works, from Kadar Asmal and Ruth First to Mandela himself, were constrained by government restrictions. Censorship, banning orders, and general restrictions on free speech set by the apartheid government constrained and prevented many works from publication or circulation in South Africa. Mandela, moreover, could not speak publicly, be quoted, or have any of his writings published within South Africa for most of his life until 1989. Even his autobiography had to be smuggled out of prison in various parts and then later unified and edited under the guiding hand of Richard Stengel of *Time* magazine, who was invited to assist in ghostwriting the final version of *Long Walk to Freedom*. As many biographers, and he himself noted, he sacrificed much of his personal life and family relations for the sake of the struggle. The ANC fashioned itself

along the lines of many democratic socialist organizations with firmly centralized structures of authority and an absolute demand for loyalty to doctrine and party. In this regard, Mandela's unwavering support and obedience to ANC policies and the leadership shaped much of the discourse around writings on him and the party.

Of course, among the most important insights into Mandela are to be found in the various biographies and especially in his renowned autobiography, *Long Walk to Freedom*. The autobiography, originally published in English, has already been translated into over twenty-seven different languages around the world including Arabic, Russian, Mandarin, and even Braille. In South Africa, Vivlia Publishers commissioned translations in Afrikaans, Sepedi, Sesotho, isiXhosa, and isiZulu, in part because Mandela himself wanted it to be available in the main indigenous languages of his country. There was some degree of ambiguity surrounding the Afrikaans translation of his autobiography since some viewed Afrikaans as the "language of the oppressor," while others noted that it is the first language of many Blacks in South Africa, including the vast majority of the Coloured population. *Long Walk* has its own curious history. It was, almost from inception, a collaborative effort. Mandela wrote much of it secretly on papers that were circulated and reviewed by his fellow political prisoners. Mac Maharaj then transcribed the manuscript into tiny script on scraps that could be hidden in various books that they were allowed for their college correspondence studies. These were later shipped out with Maharaj's possessions on his release from prison. Mandela ultimately collaborated with former *Time* magazine editor Richard Stengel on the final published version. It remains an international bestseller and is widely used in high schools and universities around the world for a variety of courses.

Related to his autobiography, which many historians see as a primary source, are records and accompanying analyses of various speeches by Mandela and documents related to the ANC. These document histories, including the important collection by Hunt Davis and

Sheridan Johns, as well as the various collections of Mandela's speeches, especially his *The Struggle Is My Life*, form a significant part of the archive of his life and appendix B provides excerpts from some of the most important of these.

While the biographies may not hold significant literary merit, they do provide an important body of evidence for historical analysis and corroboration, and they are vital for understanding both Mandela's historical memory and individual experiences. Indeed, the most compelling biographies were written by people who knew Mandela personally, and had shared experience of many of the critical events in his history. In this regard, most share his central political convictions and dedication to the liberation struggle. Many of them, and their writings, were also censored or banned by the South African apartheid government, in part, because of their association with the ANC and Mandela. His earliest official biographer was Mary Benson, who conducted extensive interviews with Mandela just prior to his long incarceration. Other notable biographers who worked with or knew Mandela personally include the antiapartheid activist and academic Fatima Meer, and Anthony Sampson, the former editor of *Drum* magazine. Another set of biographically related works on Mandela include insights from fellow prisoners and members of the ANC and South African Communist Party. Among the most insightful are works in this regard are writings by Mac Marharaj and Ahmed Kathrada. Others who worked closely with Mandela in various capacities, some political, some legal, and some as personal assistants also provide some keen insights in their works. George Bizos's, Mandela's longtime friend and lawyer, and Zelda la Grange's works are among the more interesting in this category.

Although this bibliography does not list many of the works that constitute what could be referred to, perhaps somewhat disingenuously, as political propaganda, they remain, in various forms, an important dimension of the way his life has been represented. Since the 1960s when his long incarceration began, the emergent global antiapartheid movement cultivated images and stories about Mandela as the central symbols of the effort to end the racist oppression and exploitation of Blacks not only in South Africa, but in many countries. In addition to the numerous pamphlets, magazines, and advocacy pieces, photo essays on Mandela, his life and times, became inspiring contributions to the archive of his life. In addition to *Drum* magazine, the photographic work and essays of Peter Magubane and Jürgen Schadeberg were important for shaping the global image of Nelson Mandela. A further exploration of Mandela's heroic image can be seen in the popular *Nelson Mandela: The Authorised Comic Book*.

Finally, with the prolific expansion of the worldwide Internet, I have provided a limited number of what I believe to be the best and well-supported, stable, web-based sources that provide ready access to a remarkable number of materials written, audible and visual.

GENERAL

Beinart, William. *Twentieth-Century South Africa*. Oxford: Oxford University Press, 2001.

Berger, Nathan. *Chapters from South African History, Jewish and General*. Johannesburg: Kayor, 1982.

Berger, Peter L., and Bobby Godsell, eds. *A Future South Africa: Visions, Strategies, and Realities*. Boulder, CO: Westview Press, 1988.

Davenport, Rodney, and Christopher Saunders. *South Africa: A Modern History*, fifth edition. New York: Macmillan, 2000.

Giliomee, Hermann, and Bernard Mbenga. *A New History of South Africa*. Cape Town: Tefelburg, 2007.

MacKinnon, Aran. *The Making of South Africa: Culture and Politics*, second edition. Hoboken, NJ: Pearson, 2012.

Omer-Cooper, John. *History of Southern Africa*, second edition. Portsmouth, NH: Heinemann, 1994.

Ross, Robert. *A Concise History of South Africa*. Cambridge: Cambridge University Press, 1999.

Ross, Robert, Anne Mager, and Bill Nasson, eds. *The Cambridge History of South Africa*, volume 2. Cambridge: Cambridge University Press, 2011.

Saunders, Christopher, ed. *Readers Digest Illustrated History of South Africa*. London and New York: The Reader's Digest Association, 1994.

Shillington, Kevin. *History of Southern Africa*. Edinburgh: Longman, 1997.

Thompson, Leonard. *A History of South Africa*, third edition. New Haven, CT: Yale University Press, 2001.

Wilson, Monica, and Leonard Thompson. *The Oxford History of South Africa*, two volumes. Oxford: Oxford University Press 1969, 1971.

Worden, Nigel. *The Making of Modern South Africa*. Oxford: Oxford University Press, 1994.

POLITICS

Adam, Heribert, and Hermann Giliomee. *Ethnic Power Mobilized*. New Haven, CT: Yale University Press, 1979.

Adam, Heribert, and Kogila Moodley. *The Negotiated Revolution: Society and Politics in Post-Apartheid South Africa*. Johannesburg: Ball, 1993.

Alden, Chris. *Apartheid's Last Stand. The Rise and Fall of the South African Security State*. London: Macmillan, 1996.

Andrews, Penelope, and Stephen Elleman, eds. *The Post-Apartheid Constitutions*. Johannesburg: University of Witwatersrand Press, 2001.

Breytenbach, Cloete. *The New South Africa: The Zulu Factor*. Montagu, South Africa: Luga, 1991.

Cohen, Robin, Yvonne Muthien, and Abede Zegeye, eds. *Repression and Resistance: Insiders' Accounts of Apartheid*. London: Zell, for the Centre for Modern African Studies, 1990.

Davenport, Rodney. *The Birth of a New South Africa/The Transfer of Power in South Africa*. London: Heinemann, 1998.

De Klerk, Fredrick. *The Last Trek: A New Beginning*. London and Johannesburg: Macmillan, 1998.

Ellis, Stephen, and Tsepo Sechaba. *Comrades Against Apartheid: The ANC and the South African Communist Party in Exile*. Bloomington: Indiana University Press, 1992.

Gastrow, Shelagh. *Who's Who in South African Politics*, number 5. Randburg, South Africa: Raven Press, 1995.

Guelke, Adrian. *Rethinking the Rise and Fall of Apartheid: South Africa and World Politics*. New York: Palgrave Macmillan, 2005.

Halisi, C. R. D. *Black Political Thought in the Making of South African Democracy*. Bloomington: Indiana University Press, 2000.

Hanlon, Joseph. *Apartheid's Second Front: South Africa's War Against Its Neighbours*. New York: Penguin, 1986.

———. *South Africa: The Sanctions Report*. London: Heinemann, 2005.

Harvey, Robert. *The Fall of Apartheid: The Inside Story from Smuts to Mbeki*. New York: Palgrave, 2001.

James, Wilmot. *After the TRC: Reflections on Truth and Reconciliation in South Africa*. Athens: Ohio University Press, 2000.

Johnson, Robert. *South Africa's Brave New World. The Beloved Country Since the End of Apartheid*. New York: The Overlook Press, 2013.

Juckes, Tim. *Opposition in South Africa: The Leadership of Z. K. Matthews, Nelson Mandela, and Stephen Biko*. Westport, CT: Praeger, 1995.

Kathrada, Ahmed. *No Bread for Mandela: Memoirs of Ahmed Kathrada, Prisoner No. 468/64*. Lexington: University of Kentucky Press, 2011.

Lodge, Tom. *Black Politics in South Africa since 1945*. Johannesburg: Raven Press, 1983.

———. *South African Politics Since 1994*. Cape Town: David Phillip, 1999.

———. *Politics in South Africa: from Mandela to Mbeki*. Bloomington: Indiana University Press, 2002.

Marais, Hein. *South Africa: Limits to Change—The Political Economy of Transition.* London: Zed, 1998.

Matanzima, Kaiser Daliwonga. *Independence My Way.* Pretoria: Foreign Affairs Association, 1976.

Mermelstein, David, ed. *The Anti-Apartheid Reader.* New York: Grove Press, 1987.

O'Meara, Dan. *Forty Lost Years: The Apartheid State and the Politics of the National Party, 1948–94.* Athens: Ohio University Press, 1996.

Reynolds, Andrew. *Election '99 South Africa.* New York: A. Knopf, 1999.

Schadeberg, Jurgen. *Voices from Robben Island.* Johannesburg: Raven Press, 1994.

Temkin, Ben. *Buthelezi: A Biography.* London: Routledge, 2003.

van Kessel, Ineke. *"Beyond Our Wildest Dreams": The United Democratic Front and the Transformation of South Africa.* Charlottesville: University of Virginia Press, 2000.

HISTORY

Alexander, Neville. *Robben Island Prison Dossier 1964–1974.* Rondebosch: University of Cape Town, 1994.

Beinart, William. *The Political Economy of Pondoland.* Cambridge: Cambridge University Press 1982.

———. *Settlers, Livestock and the Cape Environment, c. 1770–1950.* Oxford: Oxford University Press, 2012.

Beinart, William, and Colin Bundy. *Hidden Struggles in Rural South Africa: Politics and Popular Movements in the Transkei and Eastern Cape, 1890–1930.* London: James Curry, 1987.

Beinart, William, Peter Delius, and Stanley Trapido, eds. *Putting a Plough to the Ground: Accumulation and Dispossession in Rural South Africa.* Johannesburg: Raven Press, 1986.

Beinart, William, and Saul Dubow, eds. *Segregation and Apartheid in Twentieth-Century South Africa.* London: Routledge, 1995.

Benson, Mary. *African Patriots: The Story of the African National Congress of South Africa.* London: Faber and Faber, 1963.

———. *South Africa: The Struggle for a Birthright.* London: Penguin, 1966.

Bergh, John S., and Jan C. Visagie. *The Eastern Cape Frontier Zone, 1660–1980: A Cartographic Guide for Historical Research.* Durban: Butterworths, 1985.

Beukes, Piet. *The Religious Smuts.* Cape Town: Human and Rousseau, 1994.

Bickford-Smith, Vivian. "South African Urban History, Racial Segregation and the 'Unique' Case of Cape Town?" *Journal of Southern African Studies* [Oxford] 21, no. 1 (March 1995): 63–78.

Bonner, Philip L. *Kings, Commoners, and Concessionaires: The Evolution and Dissolution of the Nineteenth-Century Swazi State.* New York: Cambridge University Press, 1983.

Bonner, Philip, Peter Delius, and Deborah Posel, eds. *Apartheid's Genesis.* Johannesburg: Raven, 1993.

Bouch, Richard. "Glen Grey Before Cecil Rhodes: How a Crisis of Local Colonial Authority Led to the Glen Grey Act of 1894." *Canadian Journal of African Studies* [Toronto] 27, no. 1 (Winter 1993): 1–24.

Bradford, Helen. *A Taste of Freedom: The ICU in Rural South Africa, 1929–30.* New Haven, CT: Yale University Press, 1987.

Bundy, Colin. *The Rise and Fall of the South African Peasantry.* London: James Curry, 1979.

Buntman, Fran. *Robben Island and Prisoner Resistance to Apartheid.* New York: Cambridge University Press, 2003.

Callinicos, Luli. *Oliver Tambo: Beyond the Engeli Mountains.* Claremont, South Africa: David Philip, 2004.

Carton, Benjamin. *Blood from Your Children: The Colonial Origins of Generational Conflict in South Africa.* Pietermaritzburg: University of KwaZulu-Natal Press, 2000.

Cell, John. *The Highest Stage of White Supremacy: The Origins of Segregation in*

South Africa and the American South. New Haven, CT: Yale, 1982.

Clingman, Stephen. *Bram Fischer: Afrikaner Revolutionary.* Boston: University of Massachusetts Press, 1998.

Cobbing, Julian. "The Mfecane as Alibi: Thoughts on Dithakong and Mbolompo." *Journal of African History* 29 (1988).

Cope, Nicholas. *To Bind the Nation: Solomon Kadinuzulu and Zulu Nationalism, 1913–1933.* Pietermaritzburg: University of Natal Press, 1993.

Cope, Richard. *The Ploughshare of War: The Origins of the Anglo-Zulu War of 1879.* Scottsville: University of Kwa-Zulu-Natal Press, 1999.

Crais, Clifton. *White Supremacy and Black Resistance in Pre-Industrial South Africa: The Making of the Colonial Order in the Eastern Cape, 1770–1868,* Cambridge: Cambridge University Press, 1992.

Crush, Jonathan, Alan Jeeves, and David Yudelman. *South Africa's Labour Empire: A History of Black Migrancy to the Gold Mines.* Montreal: McGill University Press, 1991.

Dubow, Saul. *Racial Segregation and the Origins of Apartheid in South Africa, 1910–1936.* London: James Curry, 1989.

———. *The African National Congress.* Gloucester: Stroud, 2000.

———. *Apartheid: 1948–1994.* Oxford: Oxford University Press, 2014.

Duminy, Andrew, and Bill Guest, eds. *Natal and Zululand. From Earliest Times to 1910.* Pietermaritzburg: University Of Natal Press, 1989.

Elphick, Richard. *KhoiKhoi and the Founding of White South Africa.* Johannesburg: Raven Press, 1985.

Elphick, Richard, and Rodney Davenport, eds. *Christianity in South Africa: A Political, Social and Cultural History.* Berkeley: University of California Press, 1997.

Elphick, Richard, and Hermann Giliomee, eds. *The Shaping of South African Society, 1652–1840.* Cape Town: David Phillip, 1989.

Etherington, Norman. *The Great Treks: The Transformation of Southern Africa, 1815–1854.* London: Macmillan, 2001.

Gerhart, Gail. *Black Power in South Africa: The Evolution of an Ideology.* Berkeley: University of California Press, 1979.

Giliomee, Hermann. *Afrikaner Political Thought.* Cape Town: University of Cape Town Press, 1983.

Guy, Jeff. *The Destruction of the Zulu Kingdom: The Civil War in Zululand, 1879–84.* London: Longman, 1983.

Hamilton, Carolyn. *The Mfecane Aftermath: Reconstructive Debates in Southern African History.* Johannesburg: University of the Witwatersrand Press, 1995.

Holland, Heidi. *The Struggle: A History of the African National Congress.* New York: George Braziller, Inc., 1990.

Jacobs, Sean, and Richard Calland, eds. *Thabo Mbeki's World: The Politics and Ideology of the South African President.* Pietermaritzburg, South Africa: University of Natal Press, 2002.

Jeeves, Alan. *Migrant Labour in South Africa's Mining Economy: The Struggle for the Gold Mines Labour Supply, 1890–1920.* Kingston, ON: Queen's University Press, 1985.

Jordan, Pallo, and Mac Maharaj. "South Africa and the Turn to Armed Resistance." *South African Historical Journal* 70, no. 1 (2018): 11–26.

Karis, Tom, and Gwendolyn Carter. *From Protest to Challenge: Documents of African Politics in South Africa, 1882–90.* Bloomington: Indiana University Press, 1972–97.

Keegan, Timothy. *Colonial South Africa and the Origins of the Racial Order.* Charlottesville: University of Virginia Press, 1996.

Luthuli, Albert. *Let My People Go: An Autobiography.* London: Macmillan, 1962.

Mandela, Zindzi, and Peter Magubane. *Black As I Am.* Los Angeles, CA: Guild of Tutors Press, 1978.

Mare, Gerhard, and Georgina Hamilton. *An Appetite for Power: Buthelezi's Inkatha and South Africa.* Johannesburg: Raven, 1987.

Mbeki, Govan. *The Peasant's Revolt.* London, Penguin Library, 1964.

———. *Learning from Robben Island: The Prison Writings of Govan Mbeki.* London: James Currey, 1991.

McAllister, Patrick. *Xhosa Beer Drinking Rituals: Power Practice and Performance in the South African Periphery.* Durham, NC: Carolina Academic Press, 2006.

Meli, Francis. *A History of the ANC. South Africa Belongs to Us.* Bloomington: Indiana University Press, 1988.

Meredith, Martin. *Fischer's Choice: A Life of Bram Fischer.* Johannesburg: Jonathan Ball Publishers, 2002.

Mostert, Noel. *Frontiers: The Epic of South Africa's Creation and the Tragedy of the Xhosa People.* New York, Alfred A. Knopf, 1992.

O'Malley, Padraig. *Shades of Difference: Mac Maharaj and the Struggle for South Africa.* New York: Penguin, 2007.

Pallo, Jordan, Z. *Oliver Tambo Remembered.* Johannesburg: Pan Macmillan, 2007.

Schreiner, Else. *Time Stretching Fear: The Detention and Solitary Confinement of 14 Anti-apartheid Trialists 1987–1991.* Cape Town: Waterfront and Robben Island Museum, 2000.

Suttner, Raymond. *The ANC Underground in South Africa, 1950–1976.* Boulder, CO: First Forum Press, 2009.

Switzer, Les. *Power and Resistance in an African Society: The Ciskei Xhosa and the Making of South Africa.* Madison: University of Wisconsin Press, 1993.

Tambo, Oliver, and Enuga Reddy. *Oliver Tambo and the Struggle Against Apartheid.* New Delhi: Sterling Publishers, in collaboration with the Namedia Foundation, 1988.

Tambo, Oliver, and Adelaide Tambo. *Preparing for Power: Oliver Tambo Speaks.* New York: George Braziller, 1988.

Walker, Eric. *A History of Southern Africa.* London: Longman, 1962.

Walshe, Peter. *The Rise of African Nationalism in South Africa: The African National Congress, 1912–1952.* Berkeley: University of California Press, 1971.

Wilson, Francis. *Labour in the South African Gold Mines, 1911–1969.* Cambridge: Cambridge University Press, 1972.

Wilson, Monica Hunter, and Leonard M. Thompson, eds. *The Oxford History of South Africa,* 2 vols. New York: Oxford University Press, 1969, 1971.

Worden, Nigel. *Slavery in Dutch South Africa.* African Studies Series, No. 44. New York: Cambridge University Press, 1985.

———. *The Making of Modern South Africa: Conquest, Segregation, and Apartheid,* second edition. MA: Blackwell, 1995.

Worger, William H. *South Africa's City of Diamonds: Mine Workers and Monopoly Capitalism in Kimberley, 1867–1895.* New Haven, CT: Yale University Press, 1987.

WORKS ON NELSON MANDELA, HIS LIFE AND CAREER

Asmal, Kadar, David Chidester, Wilmot James, eds. *Nelson Mandela in His Own Words.* New York: Little Brown, 2018.

Barber, James. *Mandela's World: The International Dimension of South Africa's Political Revolution 1990–99.* Athens: Ohio University Press, 2004.

Benson, Mary. *On Trial for Their Lives: The Accused at Rivonia.* London: Africa Bureau, 1964.

———. *Nelson Mandela.* London: Panaf Books, 1980.

———. *Nelson Mandela: The Man and the Movement.* London: Penguin, 1986; updated 1994.

Bernstein, Hilda. *The World That Was Ours: The Story of the Rivonia Trial.* London: South African Writers, 1989.

Bizos, George. *65 Years of friendship: A Memoir of My Friendship with Nelson Mandela.* Century City, South Africa: Umuzi, 2017.

Bridgland, Fred. *Katiza's Journey: Beneath the Surface of South Africa's Shame.* London: Sidgwick & Jackson, 1997.

Broun, Kenneth. *Saving Nelson Mandela: The Rivonia Trial and the Fate of South Africa.* Oxford: Oxford University Press, 2012.

Brouwer, Erik. *Schaduwboksen, Nelson Mandela Fight!* Naarden, Netherlands: Human Sources, 2011.

Buchanan, Santa, Sahm Venter, Pitshou Mampa, and Pascal Nzoni. *President in Waiting.* Johannesburg: Umlando Wezithombe Publishing, 2006.

Carlin, John. *Playing the Enemy: Nelson Mandela and the Game That Made a Nation.* New York: Penguin, 2008.

Clark, Steve, ed. *Nelson Mandela Speaks: Forging a Democratic, Nonracial South Africa.* New York: Pathfinder, 1993.

Daniel, John. "Soldiering On: The Post-presidential Years of Nelson Mandela 1999–2005." In *Legacies of Power: Leadership Change and Former Presidents in African Politics,* edited by Roger Southall and Henning Melber. Uppsala, Sweden: Nordiska Afrikainstitutet Press, 2006.

Davis, R. Hunt, and Sheridan Johns. *Mandela, Tambo, and the African National Congress: The Struggle Against Apartheid: A Documentary Survey.* New York: Oxford University Press, 1991.

Daynes. Katie. *Nelson Mandela.* Parklands, South Africa: Jacklin, 2013.

Dugmore, Harry, Stephen Francis, and Rico Schacherl, eds. *Mandela: A Life in Cartoons.* Claremont, South Africa: David Philip, 1999.

Duke, Lynne. *Mandela's World: Mandela, Mobutu, and Me—A Newswoman's African Journey.* New York: Doubleday, 2003.

Fairhead, Tyrrel. *The Madiba Mindset: Your Own Freedom Charter.* Auckland Park, South Africa: Jacana Media, 2011.

Frankel, Glen. *Rivonia's Children.* New York: Farrar, Straus and Giroux, 1999.

Goldberg, Denis. *The Mission: A Life for Freedom in South Africa.* Johannesburg: STE Publishers 2010.

Gordimer, Nadine. "Mandela. What He Means to Us." *Living in Hope and History.* New York: Farrar, Straus and Giroux, 1999.

Guiloineau, Jean, and Joseph Rowe. *Nelson Mandela: The Early Life of Rolihlahla Madiba.* Berkeley, CA: North Atlantic Books, 2002.

Hatang, Sello, and Sahm Venter. *Nelson Mandela by Himself: The Authorised Book of Quotations.* Johannesburg: MacMillan, 2013.

Hepple, Bob. *Young Man with the Red Tie: A Memoir of Mandela and the Failed Revolution: 1960–1963.* Johannesburg: Jacana Media, 2013.

Holland, Heidi. *100 Years of Struggle: Mandela's ANC.* London: Penguin, 2012.

Janties, Gavin, ed. *Strengths and Convictions: The Life and Times of the South African Nobel Peace Prize Laureates: Albert Luthuli, Desmond Tutu, F. W. de Klerk, Nelson Mandela.* Oslo, Norway: Nobel Peace Center Press Publishing in collaboration with the Nobel Peace Center, 2009.

Joffe, Joel. *The State vs. Nelson Mandela: The Trial That Changed South Africa.* Oxford, UK: One World, 2007.

Joseph, Helen. *If This Be Treason: Helen Joseph's Dramatic Account of the Treason Trial, the Longest in South Africa's History and One of the Strangest Trials of the 20th Century.* Johannesburg: Quagga Publishers, 1966.

Kantor, James. *A Healthy Grave.* London: Hamish Hamilton, 1967.

Keller, Bill. *Tree Shaker: The Life of Nelson Mandela.* New York: New York Times Books, 2013.

Kumala, Alf, and Zukiswa Wanner. *8115: A Prisoner's Home.* London: Michael Joseph, 2010.

La Grange, Zelda. *Good Morning, Mr. Mandela.* New York: Viking, 2014.

Limb, Peter. *Nelson Mandela: A Biography.* Westport, CT: Greenwood Press, 2008.

Lodge, Tom. *Politics in South Africa: From Mandela to Mbeki.* Bloomington: Indiana University Press, 2002.

———. *Mandela. A Critical Life.* New York: Oxford University Press, 2006.

Madikizela-Mandela, Winnie. *491 Days: Prisoner Number 1323/69.* Athens: Ohio University Press, 2013.

Magubane, Peter, Melanie Lawrence, et al. *Man of the People: A Photographic Tribute to Nelson Mandela.* Northlands, South Africa: Pan Macmillan South Africa, 2008

Maharaj, Mac, ed. *Reflections in Prison: Voices from the South African Liberation Struggle.* Boston: University of Massachusetts Press, 2002.

Maharaj, Mac, and Ahmad Kathrada, eds. *Mandela: The Authorized Portrait.* Kansas City, MO: Andrews McNeel, 2006.

Mampa, Pitshou, and Sivuyile Matwa. *A Son of the Eastern Cape.* Johannesburg: Umlando Wezithombe Publishing, 2005.

Mandela, Winnie. *Part of My Life Went with Him.* New York: Norton, 1985.

Mangcu, Xolele, ed. *The Meaning of Mandela: A Literary and Intellectual Celebration.* Cape Town: HSRC Press, 2006.

Mathebe, Lucky. *Mandela and Mbeki: The Hero and the Outsider.* Pretoria: Unisa Press, 2012.

McCormack, William John. *In the Prison of His Days: A Miscellany for Nelson Mandela on His 70th Birthday.* Dublin, Ireland: Lilliput Press, 1988.

Meer, Fatima. *Higher Than Hope: The Authorized Biography of Nelson Mandela.* New York: Harper & Row, 1990.

Meredith, Martin. *Nelson Mandela. A Biography.* New York: St. Martin's Press, 1997.

Mungazi, Dickson. *We Shall Not Fail: Values in the National Leadership of Seretse Khama, Nelson Mandela and Julius Nyerere.* Trenton: Africa World Press, 2005.

Naidoo, Indres. *Island in Chains: Ten Years on Robben Island/Prisoner 885/63.* London: Penguin, 1982.

Ndlovu-Gatsheni, Sabelo. "From a 'Terrorist' to Global Icon: A Critical Decolonial Ethical Tribute to Nelson Rolihlahla Mandela of South Africa." *Third World Quarterly* 35, no. 6 (2014): 905–21.

———. *The Decolonial Mandela: Peace, Justice and the Politics of Life.* New York: Berghahn, 2016.

Nelson Mandela Foundation. *Nelson Mandela: The Authorized Comic Book.* Johannesburg and Cape Town: Jonathan Ball, 2008.

Ottaway, David. *Chained Together: Mandela, de Klerk, and the Struggle to Remake South Africa.* New York: Times Books, 1993.

Parkin, Kate, ed. *Mandela: The Authorised Portrait.* London: Bloomsbury, published in association with PQ Blackwell, 2006.

Reddy, Enuga, ed. *Nelson Mandela: Symbol of Resistance and Hope for a Free South Africa: Selected Speeches Since His Release.* New Delhi: Sterling Publishers, 1990.

Roberts, Jack. *Nelson Mandela: Determined to Be Free.* Brookfield, CT: Millbrook Press, 1995.

Russell, Alec. *Bring Me My Machine Gun: The Battle for the Soul of South Africa from Mandela to Zuma.* New York: Public Affairs, 2009.

Sampson, Anthony. *Mandela: The Authorized Biography.* New York: HarperCollins, 1999.

Saunders, Christopher. "Britain, the Commonwealth, and the Question of the Release of Nelson Mandela in the 1980s." *Round Table* 106, no. 6 (December 2017): 659–69.

Schadeberg, Jürgen. *Voices from Robben Island.* Johannesburg: Ravan Press, 1994.

———, ed. *Nelson Mandela and the Rise of the ANC.* Parklands, South Africa: Jonathan Ball, 1990.

Smith, David James. *Young Mandela: The Revolutionary Years.* New York: Little Brown, 2010.

Stengel, Richard. *Mandela's Way: Fifteen Lessons on Life, Love and Courage.* New York: Crown Publishers, 2009.

Steyn, Rory as told to Debora Patta. *One Step Behind Mandela.* Rivonia, South Africa: Zebra, 2000.

Streek, Barry. *Mandela Fever: Rumors of Mandela's Release, 1984 to 1988.* Cape Town: Tamberskloof, 1989.

Tlili, Mustapha, and James Derrida, eds. *For Nelson Mandela.* New York: Henry Holt, 1987.

Trapido, Anna. *Hunger for Freedom: The Story of Food in the Life of Nelson Mandela.* Auckland Park, South Africa: Jacana Media, 2008.

Verwoerd, Melanie. *Our Madiba: Stories and Reflections from Those Who Met Nelson Mandela.* Cape Town: NB Publishers, 2014.

WORKS AUTHORED OR COAUTHORED BY NELSON MANDELA

Asmal, Kadar, Wilmot James, and Nelson Mandela. *Spirit of the Nation: Reflections on South Africa's Educational Ethos.* Pretoria, South Africa: South African Department of Education, 2002.

Harker, Joseph, and Nelson Mandela. *The Legacy of Apartheid*. London: Guardian, 1994.

Kathrada, Ahmad, Nelson Mandela, and Mxolisi Mgxashe. *Robben Island: The Reunion*. Bellville, South Africa: Mayibuye, 1996.

Kathrada, Ahmad, Nelson Mandela, Walter Sisulu, and Robert D. Vassen. *Letters from Robben Island: A Selection of Ahmed Kathrada's Prison Correspondence, 1964–1989*. Cape Town: Mayibuye, 1999.

Mandela, Nelson: *We Accuse. The Trial of Nelson Mandela*. London: African National Congress, 1962.

———. *I Am Prepared To Die*. London: International Defence and Aid Fund for Southern Africa, 1979.

———. *The Struggle Is My Life*. New York: Pathfinder, 1990.

———. *Long Walk to Freedom: The Autobiography of Nelson Mandela*. New York: Little Brown, 1994.

———. *Nelson Mandela Speaks: Forging a Democratic, Nonracial South Africa*. Cape Town: David Phillip, 1994.

———. *Mandela: An Illustrated Autobiography*. New York: Little Brown, 1996.

———. *In the Words of Nelson Mandela*. London: Profile Books, 1997.

———. *No Easy Walk to Freedom*. New York: Penguin, 2002.

———. *Nelson Mandela's Favorite African Folk Tales*. New York: Norton, 2007.

———. "Forward" in Padraig O'Malley, *Shades of Difference: Mac Maharaj and the Struggle for South Africa*. New York: Penguin, 2007.

———. *Conversations with Myself*. New York: Farrar, Straus and Giroux, 2010.

———. *Selected Speeches and Writings of Nelson Mandela: The End of Apartheid in South Africa*. St. Petersburg, FL: Red and Black Publishers, 2010.

———. *Notes to the Future: Words of Wisdom*. New York: Atria Books, 2012.

———. *The Prison Letters of Nelson Mandela*. New York: Liveright, 2018.

Mandela, Nelson, and Fidel Castro. *How Far We Slaves Have Come*. College Park, GA: Pathfinder, 1991.

Mandela, Nelson, and Mandla Langa. *Nelson Mandela: Dare Not Linger—The Presidential Years*. New York: Picador, 2017.

Mandela, Nelson, and Mxolisi Mgxashe. *Robben Island: The Reunion*. Bellville, South Africa: Mayibuye Books, University of the Western Cape, 1996.

Mandela, Nelson, and the Nelson Mandela Foundation. *A Prisoner in the Garden: Photos, Letters and Notes from Nelson Mandela's 27 Years in Prison*. New York: Viking Studio, 2005.

WORKS ON AND BY MANDELA IN AFRIKAANS AND DUTCH

Barnard, Niël. *Geheime revolusie: memoires van 'n spioenbaas*. Kapstad (Cape Town): Tafelberg, 2015.

———. *Vreedsame revolusie: uit die enjinkamer van die onderhandelinge*. Kapstad (Cape Town): Tafelberg, 2017.

Boon, Rudi, ed. *Zuid-Afrika behoort aan allen die er wonen/Nelson Mandela*. Amsterdam: Mets, 1988.

Damen, Jos. *Nelson Mandela: symbool voor vrijheid en verbroedering*. Lelystad, Netherlands: IVIO-Uitgeverij, 2008.

Esterhuyse, Willie, and Gerhard Van Niekerk. *Die tronkgesprekke: Nelson Mandela en Kobie Coetsee se voorpuntdiplomasie*. Kapstad (Cape Town): Tafelberg, 2018.

Hendricks, Gertjie Billy. *Nelson Mandela, My Hero*. Retreat, South Africa: Mawethu, 1996.

Koning, Daniel. *Wij denken niet in kleur: het Zuid-Afrika van Nelson Mandela*. Amsterdam: Rap, 1990.

la Grange, Zelda. *Goeiemore, mnr. Mandela*. Johannesburg: Penguin, 2014.

Malam, John. *Die vrylating van Nelson Mandela: 11 Februarie 1990*. Parklands, South Africa: Jacklin, 2002.

Mandela, Nelson. *Lang pad na vryheid: die outobiografie van Nelson Mandela*. Florida Hills, South Africa: Vivlia, 2001.

———. *Mandela: 'n lewe*. Kapstad (Cape Town): Sunbird, 2007.

———. *Mandela, man van versoening: huldeblyk aan SA se mees geliefde seun, 1918–2013.* Kapstad (Cape Town): Media 24, 2013.

———. *Gesprekke met myself.* Kapstad (Cape Town): Lapa, 2014.

Rode, Linda, and Suzette Kotze. *Die Madibaboek: Nelson Mandela se gunsteling-stories vir kinders.* Kapstad (Cape Town): Tafelberg, 2002.

Van Kessel, Ineke. *Nelson Mandela in een notendop: (bijna) alles wat je altijd wilde weten.* Amsterdam: Bert Bakker, 2010.

WORKS BY MANDELA IN ISIXHOSA

Mandela, Nelson. *Indlela ende eya enkululekweni: imbali ebhalwe nguNelson Mandela ngobomi bakhe.* Translation by Peter T. Mtuze. Johannesburg: Vivlia, 1994.

WORKS BY MANDELA IN ISIZULU

Mandela, Nelson. *Uhambo olude oluya enkululekweni.* Translation by Bheki Z. Ntuli. Johannesburg: Vivlia, 2001.

INTERNET SOURCES

African National Congress official website
https://www.anc1912.org.za

Aluka Archive of Nelson Mandela and the Anti-Apartheid Movement
https://www.aluka.org/struggles/collection/AAM

Apartheid Museum
http://www.apartheidmuseum.org/

The British Broadcasting Corporation resources on Nelson Mandela
http://news.bbc.co.uk/2/hi/7500615.stm

Liliesleaf Farm
http://www.liliesleaf.co.za/

The Nelson Mandela Capture Site
https://www.thecapturesite.co.za/

The Nelson Mandela Foundation
https://www.nelsonmandela.org/

The Nelson Mandela House
http://www.mandelahouse.com/index.asp

The Nelson Mandela Museum
http://www.nelsonmandelamuseum.org.za/

South African History Online, "A History of Apartheid"
https://www.sahistory.org.za/article/history-apartheid-south-africa

Then University of the Western Cape Robben Island Archive and Mayibuye Center Archive
https://mayibuyearchives.org/

Index

About the Author

Dr. Aran S. MacKinnon is professor of African history, and chair of the Department of History and Geography at Georgia College. He is the former director of the Center for Interdisciplinary Studies and of Global Studies at the University of West Georgia. He earned his PhD in history from the Institute of Commonwealth Studies at the University of London, United Kingdom; his MA in history from the University of KwaZulu-Natal, Durban, South Africa; and his BA Honors in history from Queen's University, Kingston, Canada. He has studied, worked, and taught in Canada, the United Kingdom, the United States, and South Africa and lived in Durban from 1990–1996. He is, moreover, the author of *The Making of South Africa: Culture and Politics* (second edition, 2012) as well as numerous articles on South African history in various scholarly journals; coeditor with Elaine MacKinnon of *Places of Encounter, Time, Place and Connectivity in World History*, volumes 1 and 2 (2012); and coauthor of *An Introduction to Global Studies* (2010). His primary fields of research cover the region of the old Zulu kingdom during the era of segregation in South Africa as well as work on ethnic identity and the political economy of Zululand. Most recently, he was interviewed by Jeremy Hobson of National Public Radio's *Here and Now* show about "Teaching the Lessons of Nelson Mandela."

Ingram Content Group UK Ltd.
Milton Keynes UK
UKHW051845030423
419573UK00009B/95

9 781538 122815